SQL: Fundamentals of Querying (Third Edition)

Lesson 1: Executing a Simple Query

Lesson 2: Performing a Conditional Search

Lesson 3: Working with Functions

Lesson 4: Organizing Data

About This Course

You have access to company databases and your job may require you to retrieve data from these databases. Retrieval of information from a database is dependent on precisely ordered logic and specific information. The course, *SQL: Fundamentals of Querying (Third Edition)* will help you use Structured Query Language (SQL) as a tool to implement logic and define instructions.

A database is a collection of vast information. For example, the database for a publishing company may contain information about the books, customers, orders placed, representatives, and sales. All this information is useless, unless you know how to retrieve this information and use it. Using SQL, you can retrieve this information from the database.

Course Description

Target Student

Any person with basic computer skills, familiar with concepts related to database structure and terminology, and wants to use SQL to query databases.

Course Prerequisites

The following Element K courses or equivalent knowledge are highly recommended:

- *Windows XP Professional: Level 1*
- *Windows XP Professional: Level 2*
- *Microsoft Windows Vista: Level 1*
- *Microsoft Windows Vista: Level 2*
- *Relational Databases Design (Second Edition)*
- *Access 2003: Designing a Database*

How to Use This Book

As a Learning Guide

Each lesson covers one broad topic or set of related topics. Lessons are arranged in order of increasing proficiency with *SQL: Fundamentals of Querying*; skills you acquire in one lesson are used and developed in subsequent lessons. For this reason, you should work through the lessons in sequence.

We organized each lesson into results-oriented topics. Topics include all the relevant and supporting information you need to master *SQL: Fundamentals of Querying*, and activities allow you to apply this information to practical hands-on examples.

You get to try out each new skill on a specially prepared sample file. This saves you typing time and enables you to concentrate on the skill at hand. Through the use of sample files, hands-on activities, illustrations that give you feedback at crucial steps, and supporting background information, this book provides you with the foundation and structure to learn *SQL: Fundamentals of Querying* quickly and easily.

As a Review Tool

Any method of instruction is only as effective as the time and effort you are willing to invest in it. In addition, some of the information that you learn in class may not be important to you immediately, but it may become important later on. For this reason, we encourage you to spend some time reviewing the topics and activities after the course. For additional challenge when reviewing activities, try the ″What You Do″ column before looking at the ″How You Do It″ column.

As a Reference

The organization and layout of the book make it easy to use as a learning tool and as an after-class reference. You can use this book as a first source for definitions of terms, background information on given topics, and summaries of procedures.

Course Icons

Icon	Description
	A **Caution Note** makes students aware of potential negative consequences of an action, setting, or decision that are not easily known.
	**Display Slide** provides a prompt to the instructor to display a specific slide. Display Slides are included in the Instructor Guide only.
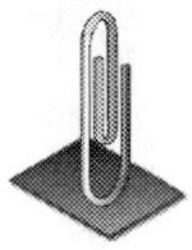	An **Instructor Note** is a comment to the instructor regarding delivery, classroom strategy, classroom tools, exceptions, and other special considerations. Instructor Notes are included in the Instructor Guide only.
	**Notes Page** indicates a page that has been left intentionally blank for students to write on.
	A **Student Note** provides additional information, guidance, or hints about a topic or task.
	A **Version Note** indicates information necessary for a specific version of software.

Course Objectives

In this course, you will learn how to compose SQL queries to retrieve information from the database.

You will:

- connect to the SQL Server database and execute a simple query.
- include a search condition in a simple query.
- use various functions based on the data types to perform calculations on data.
- organize the data obtained from the query before it is displayed on the screen.
- retrieve data from tables.
- format the output, save the result, and generate a report.

Course Requirements

Hardware

- Minimum of 512 MB of RAM for each computer.
- 40 GB or larger hard disk drive for each student and instructor computer.
- Pentium IV 800 MHz CPU or higher.
- VGA or higher resolution video card and monitor.
- Mouse or compatible tracking device.
- 12x (or faster) CD-ROM drive.
- Network adapter and network cabling.
- Display system to project the instructor's computer screen.

Software

- SQL Server Express 2005 for the instructor and each student.
- Microsoft SQL Server Management Studio Express 2005 for the instructor and each student.
- Microsoft Word 2003 or 2007 version.

Class Setup

Set Up the Instructor and Student Computers

Follow these steps to create the instructor and student computers:

1. Install Windows XP Professional with the following parameters.
    - **Computer Name:**
        - Students: ***Student** 01*, ***Student** 02*, and so on depending on the number of students in the class room.
        - Instructor: ***Instructor***
    - **Administrator Password:** ***password***
2. Install Windows XP Service Pack 2.
3. Assign the user as Administrator to the local machine.
    a. Open the **Computer Management** console.
    b. Expand **Local Users And Groups.**
    c. Click **Groups.**
    d. Double-click **Administrators.**
    e. Click **Add.**
    f. Click **Advanced.**
    g. Click **Find Now.**
    h. Select the user name for the computer.
    i. Click **OK** three times.
    j. Close **Computer Management.**

4. On the course CD-ROM, open the **085_971** folder. Then, open the **Data** folder. Run the 085971dd.exe self-extracting file located within. This will install a folder named **085971Data** on the C drive. This folder contains all the setup and data files that you will use to complete this course.

Install Microsoft .NET Framework 3.5

Download Microsoft .NET Framework 3.5 for Windows XP from the Microsoft site and perform a typical installation of Microsoft .NET Framework 3.5 accepting the default settings.

Install Microsoft Office 2007 System

Perform a Complete installation of Microsoft Office 2007 System.

Install SQL Server Express 2005

Download SQL Server Express 2005 and perform a typical installation of SQL Server Express 2005 accepting the default settings.

Install Microsoft SQL Server Management Studio Express 2005

Download Microsoft SQL Server Management Studio Express 2005 and perform a typical installation of Microsoft SQL Server Management Studio Express 2005 accepting the default settings.

Install OGCBooks Database in SQL Server 2005

1. In the **C:\085971Data** folder, open the OGCBooks.sql file in SQL Server Management Studio Express 2005 and execute the commands as per instructions given in the file.
2. Close the SQL Server Management Studio Express 2005 application.

Uncheck Hide Extensions for Known File Types

1. Open **My Computer.**
2. Choose **Tools→Folder Options.**
3. In the **Folder Options** dialog box, click the **View** tab, and verify that the **Hide extensions for known file types** check box is not checked.

List of Additional Files

Printed with each activity is a list of files students open to complete that activity. Many activities also require additional files that students do not open, but are needed to support the file(s) students are working with. These supporting files are included with the student data files on the course CD-ROM or data disk. Do not delete these files.

1 Executing a Simple Query

Lesson Time: 45 minutes

Lesson Objectives:

In this lesson, you will connect to the SQL Server database and execute a simple query.

You will:

- Connect to the database using SQL Server Management Studio Express.
- Query the database.
- Save a query for future use.
- Modify an existing query.
- Execute a saved query.

Introduction

In the *SQL: Fundamentals of Querying* course, you will query SQL database using fundamental query techniques. Simple queries form the basis of building your querying skills. In this lesson, you will begin by composing and executing a simple SQL statement to retrieve information from a database. You will then modify and save a query so that it can be used later.

Databases are designed to store a wide variety of organizational information. To use this information, you need to access the database. This means you must be familiar with the language used to communicate with databases. Writing a simple instruction using a language that the database understands will enable you to access this information.

TOPIC A

Connect to the Database

In this topic, you will execute a simple query. In order to do so, the first thing you need to do before you can get information out of a database is to connect to the server that contains the database. In this topic, you will access the database that contains the information.

The SQL server contains abundant information in the form of databases. To access this information, you need to connect to this computer using the front-end querying tool.

Tables

Tables

Definition:

A *table* is a collection of related information arranged in rows and columns. Information about each item in the collection is displayed as a row. The columns contain the same category of information for every item in the table. A table has a header row that identifies the category of information in each column.

Example: Table Containing Information

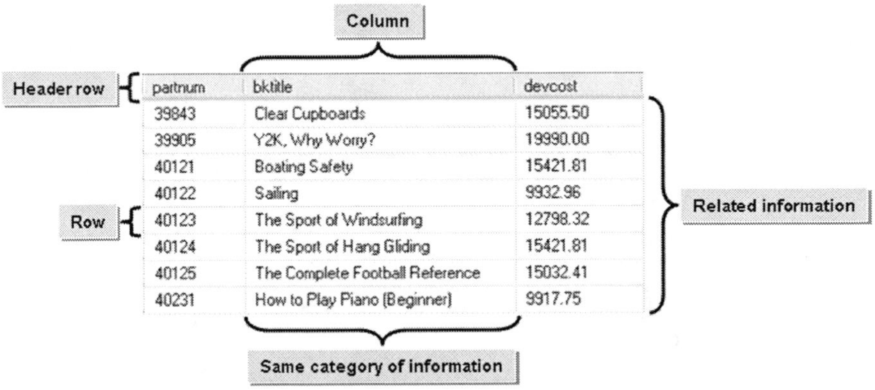

Column
Header row
Row
Related information
Same category of information
partnum bktitle devcost
39843 Clear Cupboards 15055.50
39905 Y2K, Why Worry? 19990.00
40121 Boating Safety 15421.81
40122 Sailing 9932.96
40123 The Sport of Windsurfing 12798.32
40124 The Sport of Hang Gliding 15421.81
40125 The Complete Football Reference 15032.41
40231 How to Play Piano (Beginner) 9917.75

The Database

The Database

Definition:

A *database* is a collection of information organized into objects. Information within a database is organized into one or more tables, each with a unique name. The information in the tables can be searched, retrieved, and manipulated. Some databases are created by default when the database software is installed, and others can be created and customized to suit business needs.

Example: Database Containing Information

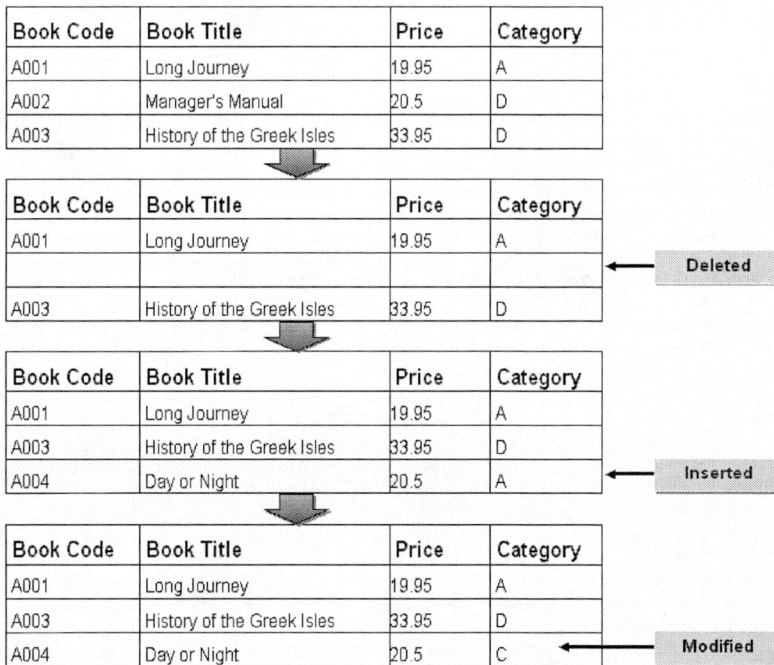

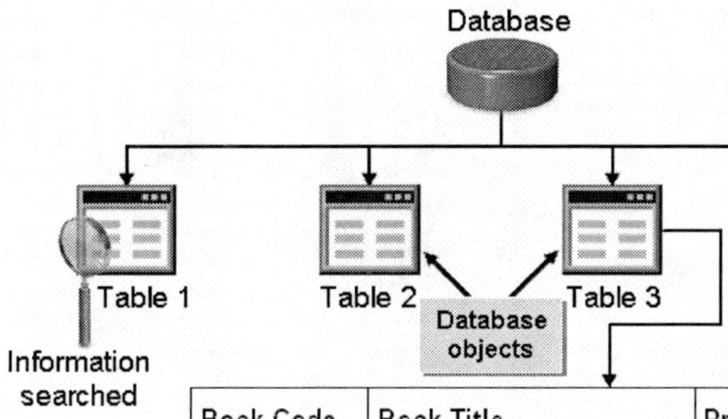

Book Code	Book Title	Price	Category
A001	Long Journey	19.95	A
A002	Manager's Manual	20.5	D
A003	History of the Greek Isles	33.95	D

Information retrieved

Example: Manipulate Information

Book Code	Book Title	Price	Category
A001	Long Journey	19.95	A
A002	Manager's Manual	20.5	D
A003	History of the Greek Isles	33.95	D

Book Code	Book Title	Price	Category
A001	Long Journey	19.95	A
				← Deleted
A003	History of the Greek Isles	33.95	D

Book Code	Book Title	Price	Category
A001	Long Journey	19.95	A
A003	History of the Greek Isles	33.95	D
A004	Day or Night	20.5	A	← Inserted

Book Code	Book Title	Price	Category
A001	Long Journey	19.95	A
A003	History of the Greek Isles	33.95	D
A004	Day or Night	20.5	C	← Modified

Example: Databases in SQL Server 2005

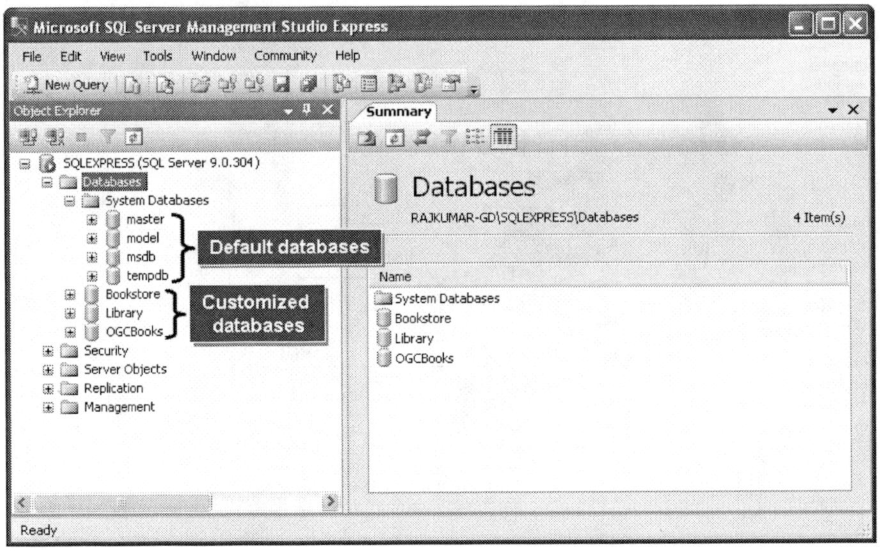

The Server

The Server

Definition:

A *server* is a computer that provides service to other computers in a network. The server may have a higher-performance capability than other computers in the network. Generally, users do not work on the servers directly. Servers manage resources and provide services to the users who access the information contained in the server.

Example: The Server Architecture

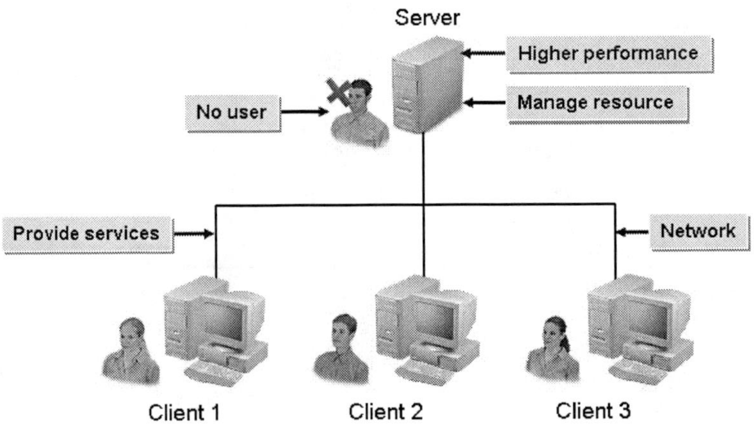

The Client

Definition:

A *client* is a computer that has the interface that enables users to request the services of the server and display the results returned by the server. The client computer has to be connected to the same network as the server to access the resources available in the server.

The Client

Example: The Client Architecture

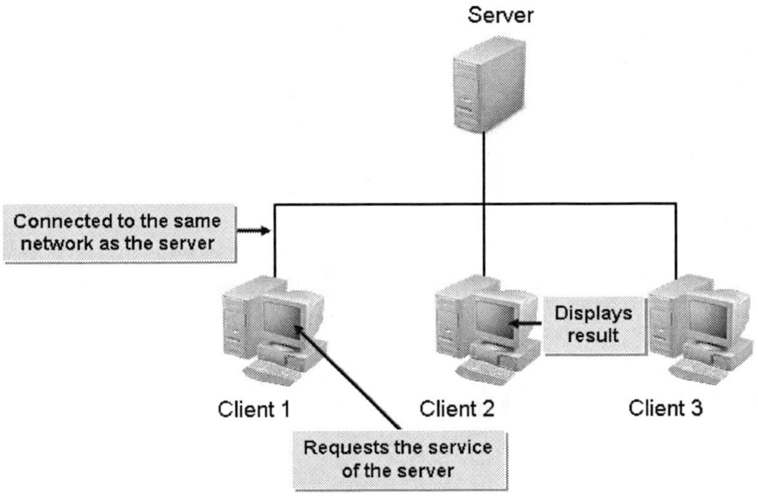

> The client/server architecture is an architecture of a computer network consisting of a server and one or more clients with the processing functions distributed between the server and the client. The client/server architecture is also referred to as two-tier architecture. The SQL Server has a client/server architecture where multiple clients and servers are allowed to transfer data over a network.

SQL

Structured Query Language (SQL) is a language used to communicate with a database. SQL consists of instructions that can be used to retrieve, modify, and delete information from the database. SQL is made up of three major language components: Data Manipulation Language (DML), Data Definition Language (DDL), and Data Control Language (DCL). So, SQL can be defined as SQL = DML + DDL + DCL.

DML is used to change or manipulate the data within a database. DML includes commands to select, update, insert, and delete data in a database. DDL is used to define the database itself. It includes clauses to create and eliminate tables, and create and eliminate views. This portion of the language is generally used by database designers. DCL is used to control access to data in a database. It includes clauses to grant and revoke database privileges. Generally, database administrators will be using this portion of the language.

SQL Language Components

The SQL language components are listed in the following table.

Table 1-1: *SQL Language Components*

DML Commands	DDL Commands	DCL Commands
`SELECT`	`CREATE TABLE`	`GRANT`
`UPDATE`	`DROP TABLE`	`REVOKE`
`INSERT`	`CREATE VIEW`	
`DELETE`	`DROP VIEW`	

The Query Editor Window

The **Query Editor** is a **Code Editor** that is being used in the SQL Server Management Studio Express to communicate with the database. The **Code Editor** replaces the **Query Analyzer** that was included in the **SQL Server 2000** version. The **Query Editor** window consists of two panes. The top pane is the **Editor** pane, where the SQL statements are entered. The bottom pane contains the **Results** pane, which displays the results of the queries, and the **Messages** tab, which displays the information about the query that is being executed.

How to Connect to the Database

Procedure Reference: Connect to a Database

To connect to a database:

1. Choose **Start→All Programs→Microsoft SQL Server 2005→SQL Server Management Studio Express** to launch SQL Server Management Studio Express.
2. In the **Connect to Server** dialog box, from the **Server type** drop-down list, select the server type.
3. Choose the server you want to connect to.
   - In the **Server name** text box, type the server name.
   - Or, from the **Server name** drop-down list, select the server name.
4. **Windows Authentication** is the default option. If the server is configured to authenticate a user name and password, select the **SQL Server Authentication** option.
5. Click **Connect** to log in to the SQL Server.
6. If you want to view the contents of the database, in the left pane, expand the database name.
7. Access the database.
   - On the **SQL Editor** toolbar, from the **Available Databases** drop-down list, select the database you want to use.
   - Or, in the **Editor** pane, type `USE` *`databasename`* and click **Execute.**
8. On the **Standard** toolbar, click **New Query** to open a new **Query Editor** window.

ACTIVITY 1-1

Connecting to the Database

Scenario:

You have joined a book publishing company, the OGC Books. The vital information about the company is stored in a SQL database called OGCBooks. This database contains information about the OGC Books customers, titles that were published by the company, obsolete titles, sales details, and sales representatives working for the company. Your day-to-day activities will require you to retrieve information from this database. For information on the tables and column names in the OGCBooks database, refer to the table structure in Appendix A.

What You Do	How You Do It
1. Launch SQL Server Management Studio Express and connect to the server.	a. Choose **Start→All Programs→Microsoft SQL Server 2005→SQL Server Management Studio Express.** b. In the **Connect to Server** dialog box, observe that **Database Engine** is selected in the **Server type** drop-down list. c. In the **Server name** drop-down list, verify that the name of the computer is automatically selected. d. Click **Connect** to connect to the server.

2. What would happen if you do not connect to your database?

a) You can access only your data.

b) You can access any data.

✓ c) You cannot access your data.

d) You can modify your data.

3. Connect to the OGCBooks database.

a. On the **Standard** toolbar, click **New Query** to open the **Query Editor** window.

b. In the **Editor** pane, type `USE OGCBooks`

c. On the **SQL Editor** toolbar, click **Execute.**

d. In the **Results** pane, observe that a message "Command(s) completed successfully." is displayed.

e. In the **Query Editor** window, click the **Close** button to close the window.

f. In the **Microsoft SQL Server Management Studio Express** dialog box, click **No.**

TOPIC B

Query the Database

In the previous topic, you learned how to connect to the server and database. Information stored in a database can be viewed and manipulated only after it is retrieved. In this topic, you will retrieve information from the database.

You are working in an organization where the information about the employees is stored in a database. For a particular business situation, you are asked to present the details about the employees. You can list this information by entering an appropriate instruction in the **Query Editor** window.

Syntax

Definition:

Syntax

Syntax is the expected form of an instruction with clauses and placeholders for the actual elements that will be used in an instruction. The clauses used in an instruction should appear in the precise order specified in the syntax.

Example: Syntax of a SQL Query Containing Various Clauses

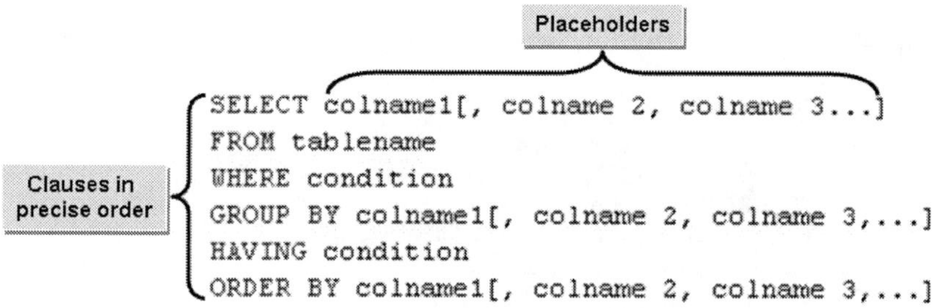
Placeholders
Clauses in precise order
SELECT colname1[, colname 2, colname 3...]
FROM tablename
WHERE condition
GROUP BY colname1[, colname 2, colname 3,...]
HAVING condition
ORDER BY colname1[, colname 2, colname 3,...]

SQL Statement

Definition:

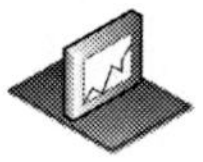

SQL Statement

A *SQL statement* is an instruction written in SQL using an appropriate syntax. The essential clauses and keywords present in a syntax have to be used when framing a SQL statement. Optional clauses can be used if required. A SQL statement is used to retrieve or manipulate the information present in the database.

Example: A SQL Statement Containing Various Clauses

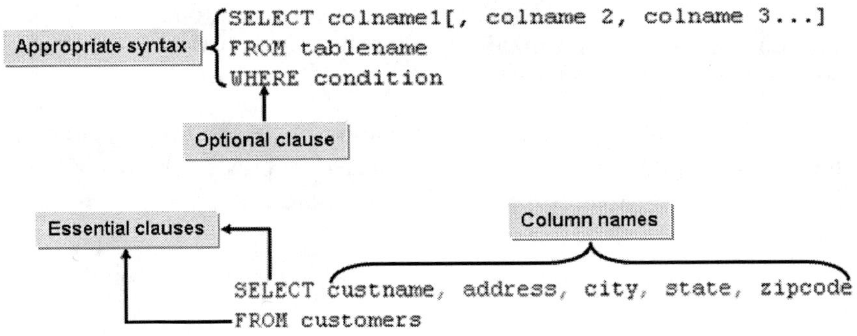
Appropriate syntax
SELECT colname1[, colname 2, colname 3...]
FROM tablename
WHERE condition
Optional clause
Essential clauses
Column names
SELECT custname, address, city, state, zipcode
FROM customers

Query

Query

Definition:

A *query* is an instruction that requests information from the tables present in a database. A query requires the column and table names to generate the output. It can include conditions to retrieve specific information.

Example: A SQL Query

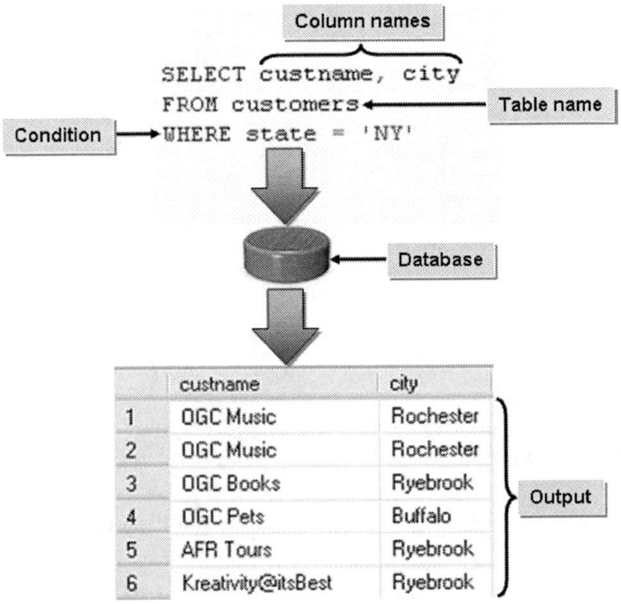
Column names
SELECT custname, city
FROM customers
Table name
Condition
WHERE state = 'NY'
Database
custname
city
1 OGC Music Rochester
2 OGC Music Rochester
3 OGC Books Ryebrook
4 OGC Pets Buffalo
5 AFR Tours Ryebrook
6 Kreativity@itsBest Ryebrook
Output

The SELECT Statement

Definition:

The SELECT Statement

The *SELECT statement* is a SQL statement used to retrieve information from a database. A simple `SELECT` statement is composed of two parts: a `SELECT` clause that includes all of the column names that are required in the output, and a `FROM` clause that contains the table name containing the columns. Additional clauses can be added to the `SELECT` statement if necessary. The order of column names used in the `SELECT` statement determines the order in which the columns are displayed in the output. When more than one column name is entered, commas are used to separate the column names. When all the columns of a table are required in the output, an asterisk (*) can be used instead of the column names.

Syntax of the SELECT Statement

```
SELECT colname1[, colname2, colname3 ...]
FROM tablename
```

In the syntax, the square parentheses [...] are used to enclose optional parameters.

```
SELECT *
FROM tablename
```

The asterisk (*) symbol is used in the `SELECT` clause to retrieve all of the columns from a table.

> The instruction used in SQL is not case sensitive. To differentiate the keywords from other words used in the instruction, keywords can be capitalized.

Example: A SELECT Statement to List Specific Columns

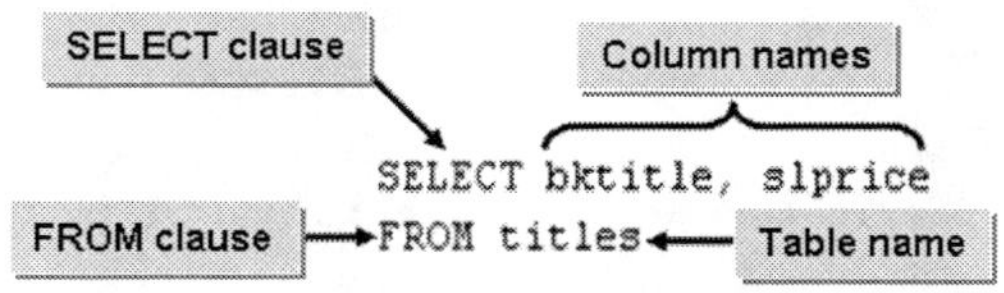

Example: A SELECT Statement to Display All Columns

```
SELECT *   ← Returns all columns from titles table
FROM titles
```

	partnum	bktitle	devcost	slprice	pubdate
1	39843	Clear Cupboards	15055.50	49.95	2005-08-19 00:00:00
2	39905	Y2K, Why Worry?	19990.00	45.00	2006-01-01 00:00:00
3	40121	Boating Safety	15421.81	36.50	2006-05-18 00:00:00
4	40122	Sailing	9932.96	29.15	2006-05-03 00:00:00
5	40123	The Sport of Windsurfing	12798.32	38.50	2005-07-13 00:00:00
6	40124	The Sport of Hang Gliding	15421.81	49.68	2006-01-06 00:00:00
7	40125	The Complete Football Reference	15032.41	49.99	2005-08-03 00:00:00
8	40231	How to Play Piano (Beginner)	9917.75	25.00	2005-06-11 00:00:00
9	40232	How to Play Piano (Intermediate)	8565.35	20.50	2005-10-22 00:00:00
10	40233	How to Play Piano (Advanced)	7971.02	20.50	2005-12-01 00:00:00

Titles

Optional Clauses of the SELECT Statement

The optional clauses of the `SELECT` statement, if used, must be in a specific order. The optional clauses have their own purposes.

Optional Clause	***Purpose***
`WHERE`	A condition specifying only certain rows to be retrieved from a table.
`GROUP BY`	A column identifier used to organize data into groups.
`HAVING`	A condition that works in conjunction with GROUP BY, specifying which groups to include in the results.
`ORDER BY`	A condition that sorts query results by one or more columns.

How to Query the Database

Procedure Reference: Query a Database

To query a database:

1. Launch SQL Server Management Studio Express.
2. Select the database that you want to use.
3. Open the **Query Editor** window.
4. In the **Editor** pane, enter the `SELECT` statement to display the desired information from a table.
5. Click **Execute.**
6. In the **Results** pane, select the **Messages** tab to view the information about the query you just executed.

ACTIVITY 1-2

Querying the Database

Scenario:

The sales manager wants to hand out a list of available book titles published in the company to a sales representative who has just joined the organization. You are asked to list the book titles that were published by the OGC Books company. You know that the information is contained in the OGCBooks database but are not aware of the tables or the contents in the database. For information on the tables and column names in the OGCBooks database, refer to the table structure in Appendix A.

What You Do	How You Do It
1. Identify the table that contains the information about the book titles published by OGC Books.	a. In the **Microsoft SQL Server Management Studio Express** window, in the **Object Explorer** pane, expand **Databases.**
	b. In the **Databases** folder, first expand **OGCBooks, Tables, dbo.Titles,** and then **Columns** to view the columns contained in the table.
	c. Verify that the **Columns** folder contains **bktitle (nvarchar(40), null).**
	d. In the **Object Explorer** pane, click the **Close** button to close the pane.

2. Enter a query to display the book titles and run the query.	a. On the **Standard** toolbar, click **New Query.**
	b. On the **SQL Editor** toolbar, from the **Available Databases** drop-down list, select **OGCBooks.**
	c. In the **Editor** pane, type **`SELECT * FROM titles`** and press **Enter.**
	d. Observe that the keywords are displayed in blue and the table name is displayed in black.
	e. On the **SQL Editor** toolbar, click **Execute** to execute the query.
	f. In the **Results** pane, observe that the part number along with the book title, development cost, sale price, and publishing date are displayed.
	You will need to scroll down to view all the rows.
	g. In the **Results** pane, select the **Messages** tab to view the information about the query that was executed.

TOPIC C

Save a Query

In the previous topic, you retrieved data from the database. Some queries may be used repeatedly on the job. In this topic, you will save a query for future use.

In the business world, many queries are lengthy and complex, and once they are created and tested, they are often reused for other purposes. The long hours spent in customizing a query are not wasted if the query is saved in a SQL file. This saves you the time of retyping the query the next time a similar output is required.

How to Save a Query

Procedure Reference: Save a Query

To save a query:

1. Open the **Save File As** dialog box.
   - Choose **File→Save.**
   - On the **Standard** toolbar, click the **Save Query** button.
   - Press **Ctrl+S.**
   - Or, right-click the **Query Editor** tab and choose **Save SQLQuery.**
2. In the **Save File As** dialog box, navigate to the folder where you want to save the file.
3. In the **File name** text box, enter a valid file name.
4. From the **Save as type** drop-down list, select **SQL files (*.sql)**
5. If necessary, close the **Query Editor** window.

ACTIVITY 1-3

Saving a Query

Scenario:

After some trial and error, you have customized the query to retrieve information about books from the database. You then realize that most of the people in the organization frequently request the information retrieved by this query. Instead of retyping this query each time this result is requested, it will be helpful if this query is saved as a SQL file. For information on the tables and column names in the OGCBooks database, refer to the table structure in Appendix A.

What You Do	How You Do It
1. Save the query as ***My First SQL*** and close the **Query Editor** window.	a. On the **Standard** toolbar, click the **Save** button.
	b. In the **Save File As** dialog box, navigate to the **C:\085971Data\Executing a Simple Query** folder.
	c. In the **File name** text box, double-click and type ***My First SQL***
	d. In the **Save as type** drop-down list, verify that the **SQL files (*.sql)** option is selected.
	e. Click the **Save** button to save the query.
	f. In the **Query Editor** window, click the **Close** button to close the window.

2. **True or False? A saved query is automatically named after the database table name that is being queried.**

   __ True

   ✓ False

TOPIC D
Modify a Query

In the previous topic, you saved a query. After you have retrieved information from the database, you can reuse the same statement to modify it according to your requirement to get the desired output. In this topic, you will modify an existing query and include comments in the Query Editor window.

You retrieve some data from the database, then realize that you did not get all the information you needed. Rather than typing a new statement all over again, you can just make a few changes in the statement you have already saved. By modifying the portions of the query to suit the current requirements, the required output can be obtained.

The Data Type

The Data Type

Definition:

Data type is a classification of data into groups based on their characteristics. The characteristics can include how many characters the value contains, whether it is a number or text, or whether it includes a decimal. The data type determines what calculations can be performed with that data. All values entered into a SQL database can be classified into one of the data types available in MS SQL 2005. The data type of the value entered into a column must match the data type that has been assigned to that column.

Example: Structure of a Table in SQL

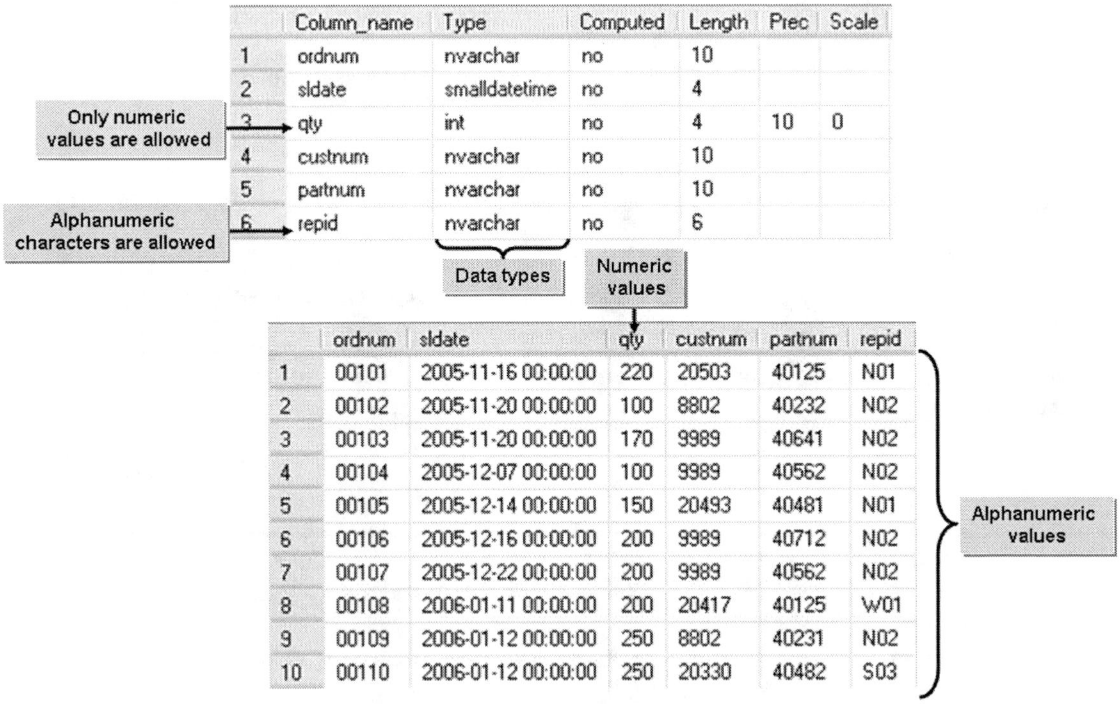

	Column_name	Type	Computed	Length	Prec	Scale
1	ordnum	nvarchar	no	10		
2	sldate	smalldatetime	no	4		
3	qty	int	no	4	10	0
4	custnum	nvarchar	no	10		
5	partnum	nvarchar	no	10		
6	repid	nvarchar	no	6		

	ordnum	sldate	qty	custnum	partnum	repid
1	00101	2005-11-16 00:00:00	220	20503	40125	N01
2	00102	2005-11-20 00:00:00	100	8802	40232	N02
3	00103	2005-11-20 00:00:00	170	9989	40641	N02
4	00104	2005-12-07 00:00:00	100	9989	40562	N02
5	00105	2005-12-14 00:00:00	150	20493	40481	N01
6	00106	2005-12-16 00:00:00	200	9989	40712	N02
7	00107	2005-12-22 00:00:00	200	9989	40562	N02
8	00108	2006-01-11 00:00:00	200	20417	40125	W01
9	00109	2006-01-12 00:00:00	250	8802	40231	N02
10	00110	2006-01-12 00:00:00	250	20330	40482	S03

Data Types Available in SQL Server

The SQL Server data types are listed in the following table.

Table 1-2: Data Types

Data Type	Used To Store
bigint	Integer (whole number) data range from –2^63 (–9,223,372,036,854,775,808) through 2^63–1 (9,223,372,036,854,775,807) with a storage size of 8 bytes.
int	Integer (whole number) data range from –2^31 (–2,147,483,648) through 2^31 – 1 (2,147,483,647) with a storage size of 4 bytes.
smallint	Integer data range from –2^15 (–32,768) through 2^15 – 1 (32,767) with a storage size of 2 bytes.
tinyint	Integer data range from 0 through 255 with a storage size of 1 byte.
bit	Integer data type that can take a value of 1, 0, or NULL.
decimal	Fixed precision and scale numeric data from –10^38 +1 through 10^38 –1.
numeric	Functionally equivalent to decimal.
money	Monetary data values range from –2^63 (–922,337,203,685,477.5808) through 2^63 – 1 (+922,337,203,685,477.5807), with accuracy to a ten-thousandth of a monetary unit with storage size of 8 bytes.
smallmoney	Monetary data values range from –214,748.3648 through +214,748.3647, with accuracy to a ten-thousandth of a monetary unit with storage size of 4 bytes.
float	Floating precision number data with the following valid values: –1.79E + 308 through –2.23E – 308, 0 and 2.23E + 308 through 1.79E + 308.
real	Floating precision number data with the following valid values: –3.40E + 38 through –1.18E – 38, 0 and 1.18E – 38 through 3.40E + 38.
datetime	Date and time data from January 1, 1753, through December 31, 9999, with an accuracy of three-hundredths of a second, or 3.33 milliseconds.
smalldatetime	Date and time data from January 1, 1900, through June 6, 2079, with an accuracy of one minute.
char	Fixed-length non-Unicode character data with a maximum storage size of 8,000 bytes.
varchar	Variable-length non-Unicode data with a maximum storage size of 8,000 bytes.
varchar(max)	Variable-length non-Unicode data with a maximum storage size of 2^31–1 bytes.
nchar	Fixed-length Unicode data with a maximum length of 4,000 characters.
nvarchar	Variable-length Unicode data with a maximum length of 4,000 characters. sysname is a system-supplied user-defined data type that is functionally equivalent to nvarchar(128) and is used to reference database object names.
nvarchar(max)	Variable-length Unicode data with a maximum length of 2^31–1 bytes.
binary	Fixed-length binary data with a maximum length of 8,000 bytes.
varbinary	Variable-length binary data with a maximum length of 8,000 bytes.
varbinary(max)	Variable-length binary data with a maximum length of 2^31–1 bytes.
cursor	A reference to a cursor.
sql_variant	A data type that stores values of various SQL Server-supported data types, except text, ntext, timestamp, and sql_variant.
table	A special data type used to store a result set for later processing.

Data Type	Used To Store
timestamp	A database-wide unique number that gets updated every time a row gets updated.
uniqueidentifier	A globally unique identifier (GUID).
xml	A built-in data type that stores XML documents and fragments in a SQL Server database. The stored representation of xml data type cannot exceed 2 GB.

> The text, ntext, and image data types will be replaced by varchar(max), nvarchar(max), and varbinary(max) in the SQL Server 2008 version.

View Data Types of the Columns in a Table

`SP_HELP` is used to display the column names and the data types used in a table.

For example,

```
SP_HELP customer
```

lists the structure of the `customer` table.

Comment

Comment

Definition:

A *comment* is a word or statement entered in the **Query Editor** window, and this word or statement is not meant to be executed when the query is run. Comments can be used to provide explanation about the code or to temporarily disable parts of a SQL statement. A single-line comment is indicated with two hyphens before the word from where you want to insert the comment. A comment with multiple lines can be enclosed within the `/*` and `*/` characters.

Example: Comment Multiple Lines of Code

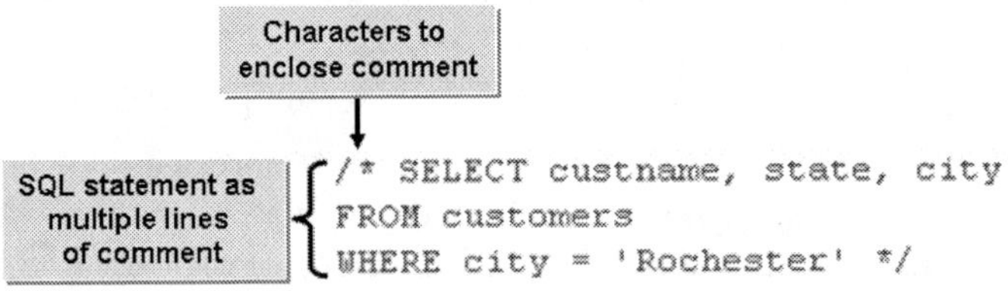
Characters to enclose comment
SQL statement as multiple lines of comment
/* SELECT custname, state, city
FROM customers
WHERE city = 'Rochester' */

Example: Comment to Provide Explanation

Explains the code

```
--Display the table structure
SP_HELP titles
```

Example: Comment Words in a Line

Comment not meant to execute

```
SELECT custname, state -- not city
FROM customers
WHERE city = 'Rochester'
```

How to Modify a Query

Procedure Reference: Modify a Query

To modify an existing query:

1. Open the saved query.
   - Choose **File→Open→File.**
   - On the **Standard** toolbar, click the **Open File** button.
   - Or, press **Ctrl+O.**
2. In the **Open File** dialog box, navigate to the desired folder and select the desired query.
3. If necessary, identify the columns required by displaying the table structure.
   a. Enter the `SP_HELP` *`tablename`* command.
   b. Select the `SP_HELP` *`tablename`* command.
   c. Click **Execute.**
4. Using the column names obtained from the table structure, modify the `SELECT` statement to display only the necessary column information.

   ```
   SELECT colname1, colname2, colname3,...FROM tablename
   ```
5. If necessary, enter a comment statement.
6. If necessary, in the **Editor** pane, comment one or more statements.
7. Click **Execute.**

ACTIVITY 1-4

Modifying a Query

Scenario:

You retrieved all the information from the "titles" table to provide the list of titles to the newly hired sales representative. After retrieving the information, you realize that there is no need to provide the sales executive with the information about development cost and published date. After displaying the table structure to retrieve column information, you realize that the statement to display the table structure is not needed. However, you do not want to delete this statement because it is used often. For information on the tables and column names in the OGCBooks database, refer to the table structure in Appendix A.

What You Do	How You Do It
1. Open the My First SQL.sql file.	a. Choose **File→Open→File.** b. In the **Open File** dialog box, navigate to the **C:\085971Data\Executing a Simple Query** folder. c. Select the **My First SQL.sql** file and click **Open** to open the query.
2. Display the table structure of the "titles" table.	a. On the **SQL Editor** toolbar, from the **Available Databases** drop-down list, select **OGCBooks.** b. In the **Editor** pane, click after `titles` and press **Enter** twice. c. Type **`SP_HELP titles`** d. On the **SQL Editor** toolbar, click **Execute** to run the query. e. On the **Messages** tab, observe that an error message is displayed.
3. Execute only the `SP_HELP titles` line to display the table structure of the "titles" table.	a. In the **Editor** pane, hold down **Shift** and click before `SP_HELP` to select the command. b. On the **SQL Editor** toolbar, click **Execute** to execute the line alone. c. In the **Results** pane, observe that the structure of the table "titles" is displayed.

4.	Enter a comment line and modify the existing query.	a. In the **Editor** pane, click in the blank space above the `SP_HELP titles` command and press **Enter.** b. Type **`--Displays the titles table structure`** c. In the `SELECT` statement, double-click `*` and press **Delete.** d. Type **`partnum, bktitle, slprice`**
5.	Save the modified query.	a. Choose **File→Save My First SQL.sql As** b. If necessary, in the **Save File As** dialog box, navigate to the **C:\085971Data\Executing a Simple Query** folder. c. In the **File name** text box, type ***Modified Query*** and then click **Save** to save the modified query. d. Close the **Query Editor** window.

TOPIC E

Execute a Saved Query

In the previous topic, you saved a query after customizing it. This saved query can be executed when a similar output is needed. In this topic, you will open and execute a saved query.

In an organization where reports are generated on a monthly basis, the queries created to generate these reports can be saved in a file so that it can be used later. The next time the same output is required, the saved file can be opened and executed to get the output for a new set of data.

How to Execute a Saved Query

Procedure Reference: Execute a Saved Query

To execute a saved query:

1. If necessary, open the **Query Editor** window by connecting to the database.
2. Open the **Open File** dialog box.
   - Choose **File→Open.**
   - On the **Standard** toolbar, click the **Open File** button.
   - Or, press **Ctrl+O.**
3. In the **Open File** dialog box, navigate to the desired folder, select the desired SQL file, and click **Open.**
4. Execute the query.

ACTIVITY 1-5

Executing a Saved Query

Scenario:

The sales manager wants an updated list of the book titles that were published by the company. You realize that you have saved the query to retrieve the book titles along with their sale price and part number in the hard drive.

What You Do	How You Do It
1. Open the saved SQL file and run the query.	a. Choose **File→Open→File.** b. If necessary, in the **Open File** dialog box, navigate to the **C:\085971Data\Executing a Simple Query** folder. c. Select the **Modified Query.sql** file and click **Open** to open the query file. d. On the **SQL Editor** toolbar, from the **Available Databases** drop-down list, select **OGCBooks.** e. Click before `SP_HELP` and type **--** f. Execute the query. g. In the **Results** pane, observe that the part number along with the book title and sale price are displayed. h. On the **Standard** toolbar, click the **Save Query** button to save the query. i. Close the **Query Editor** window.

2. **What is the first step in the procedure to execute a saved query?**

a) Navigate to the stored file.

b) Click the Open File button.

✓ c) Connect to the database.

d) Open the file directly.

Lesson 1 Follow-up

In this lesson, you connected to the computer that contains the database. You also executed a simple query and saved it. Then, you opened the query and executed it to retrieve the result. By connecting to the database, you were able to retrieve the information that is stored in it.

1. **How do you find querying helpful in your current role?**

   Answers will vary.

2. **Which language component has more usage in your current job? Why?**

   Answers will vary.

2 Performing a Conditional Search

Lesson Time: 1 hour(s), 40 minutes

Lesson Objectives:

In this lesson, you will include a search condition in a simple query.

You will:

- Use a simple search condition to retrieve the desired output.
- Compare column values.
- Search using multiple conditions.
- Retrieve records based on a range of values and null values.
- Search for patterns in a table.

Introduction

The `SELECT` statement is used to retrieve all the records contained in a database table. But, usually you don't need all that information at the same time. It's more likely that you will need to narrow down your search to specific records of interest. In this lesson, you will add additional criteria to perform a more sophisticated search.

Let's say you have a database containing information about all the employees in a company. You may need a list of just the employees in the marketing department, or the employees who joined the company between 2003 and 2006, or the employees who have been with the company for over five years and who have not utilized their full vacation time. Rather than displaying all the information in the database and then manually going through it to try to find the information you need, you can narrow down your search by mentioning the exact specification in the query.

TOPIC A

Search Using a Simple Condition

You used a simple query to retrieve all the rows of information present in the table. When you need only specific information, you need to use a criteria to retrieve the rows that are needed. In this topic, you will use simple search conditions to retrieve the necessary information.

A table in a database may contain many rows of information. If only five rows of information are required, then a search condition can be provided in a query to display only the required information.

Conditions

Conditions

Definition:

A *condition* is a search criteria used in a SQL statement to retrieve or manipulate specific information. More than one search criteria can be included in a SQL statement to retrieve the exact information. The search criteria is used to compare the information in the columns to a specific value. Calculations can also be performed on numeric columns before comparing information.

Example: Using a Condition

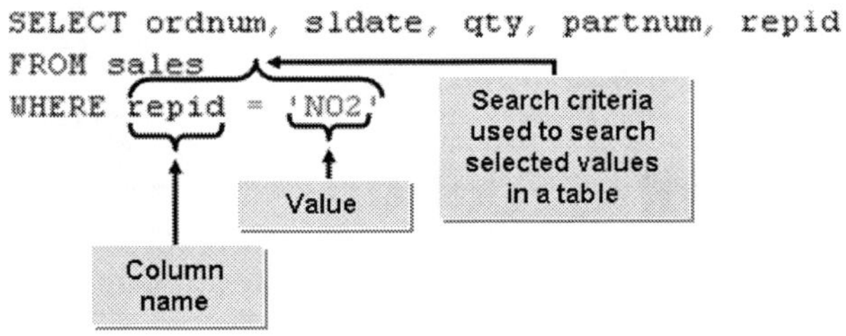
SELECT ordnum, sldate, qty, partnum, repid
FROM sales
WHERE repid = 'NO2'
Search criteria used to search selected values in a table
Value
Column name

Example: Using Multiple Conditions

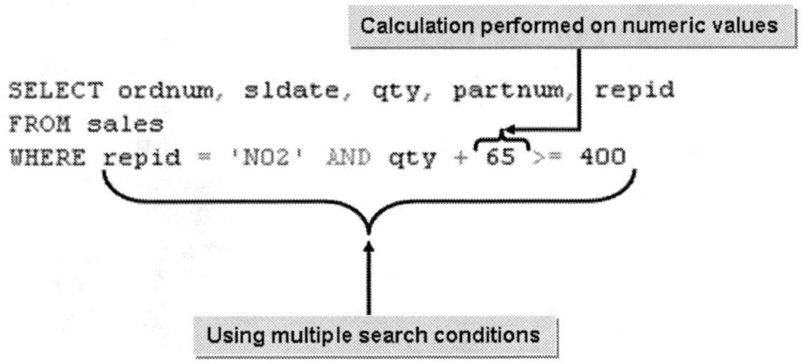
Calculation performed on numeric values
SELECT ordnum, sldate, qty, partnum, repid
FROM sales
WHERE repid = 'NO2' AND qty + 65 >= 400
Using multiple search conditions

Process of a Conditional Search

Process of a Conditional Search

In a conditional search:

1. The `SELECT` statement along with a condition is entered in the **Query Editor** window.
2. Every row in the table is searched using the condition present in the `WHERE` clause.
3. The records that match the condition are retrieved from the table.
4. The retrieved records or the output is then displayed in the **Query Editor** window.

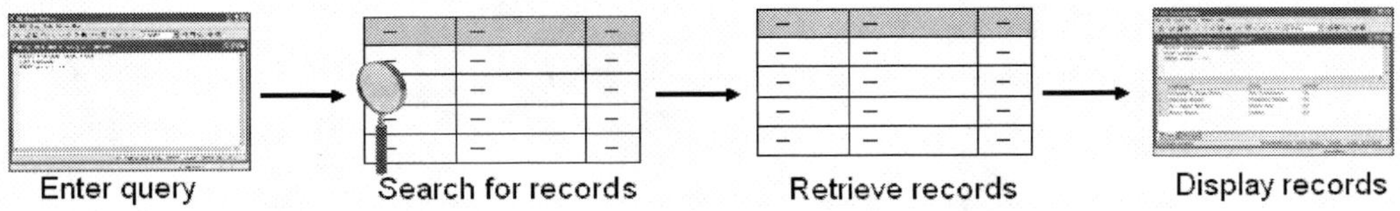

Figure 2-1: *The process of a conditional search.*

Operators

Operators

Definition:

Operators are symbols or words used in expressions to manipulate values. Operators are mostly used between a word and a value in a search criteria. Operators can be used to perform calculations, compare values, and match patterns.

Example: Operators Used in Conditions

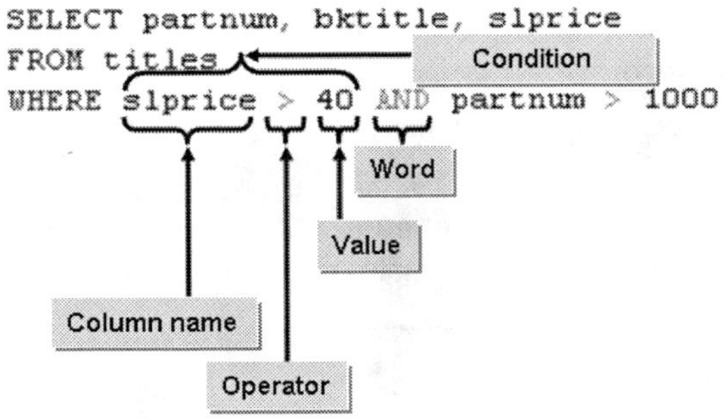

Example: Operator Used in the SELECT Statement

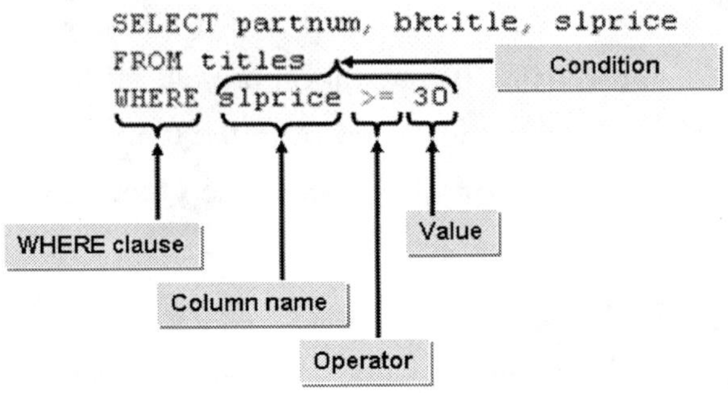
SELECT partnum, bktitle, slprice
FROM titles
WHERE slprice >= 30
Condition
WHERE clause
Column name
Operator
Value

Operators Used in SQL

There are seven categories of operators used in Microsoft® SQL Server™ 2005.

Table 2-1: *Categories of Operators*

Operator	***Description***
Arithmetic operators	Perform mathematical operations on two expressions of the numeric data type category.
Assignment operator	Establishes the relationship between a column heading and the expression that defines the values for the column.
Bitwise operators	Perform bit manipulations between two expressions of the integer data type category.
Comparison operators	Test whether two expressions are the same.
Logical operators	Test for the truth of a condition. Return a Boolean data type with a value of TRUE or FALSE.
String concatenation operator	Allows string concatenation.
Unary operators	Perform an operation on only one expression of any of the data types of the numeric data type category.

The WHERE Clause

The WHERE Clause

Definition:

The *WHERE clause* is a clause that specifies a condition in a SQL statement. The `WHERE` clause contains the expression or column name followed by an operator, and then by an expression or value that needs to be compared. More than one condition can be included in the `WHERE` clause.

Syntax of the WHERE Clause Used in the SELECT Statement

```
SELECT colname1[, colname2, colname3 ...]
FROM tablename
WHERE condition
```

Example: A WHERE Clause with One Condition

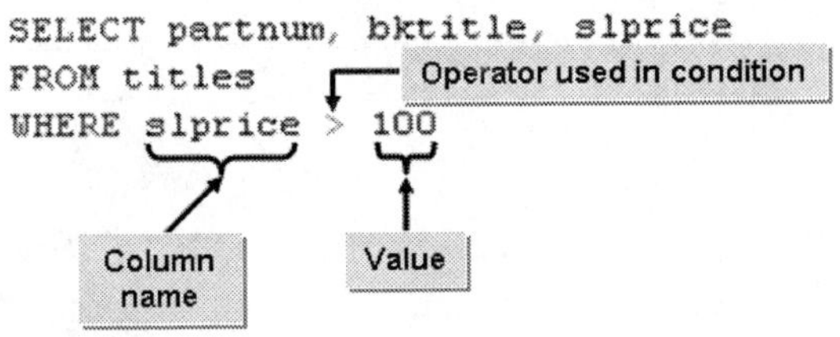

Example: A WHERE Clause with More than One Condition

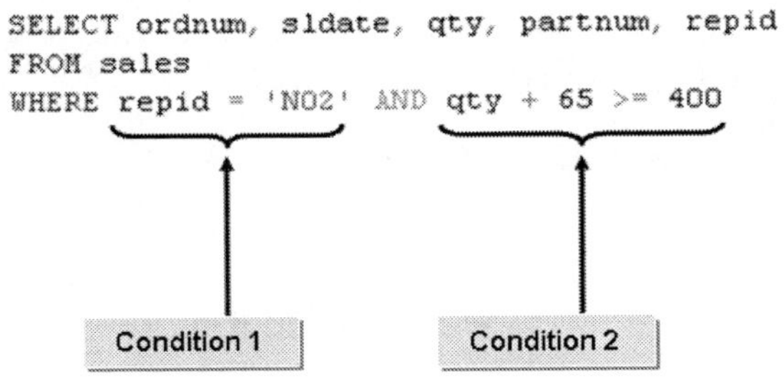

SELECT ordnum, sldate, qty, partnum, repid
FROM sales
WHERE repid = 'NO2' AND qty + 65 >= 400
Condition 1
Condition 2

How to Search Using a Simple Condition

Procedure Reference: Search Using a Simple Condition

To search using a simple condition:

1. Enter the `SELECT` clause followed by the column names.
2. Enter the `FROM` clause followed by the table name.
3. Enter the `WHERE` clause followed by a condition.
    a. Enter the column name that is present in the table.
    b. Enter a comparison operator.
    c. Enter the value of the column to be compared with.
4. Click **Execute.**

ACTIVITY 2-1

Searching Using a Simple Condition

Before You Begin:

1. On the **Standard** toolbar, click **New Query** to open the **Query Editor** window.
2. On the **SQL Editor** toolbar, ensure that the OGCBooks database is selected from the **Available Databases** drop-down list.

Scenario:

The accounts department wants to analyze the increasing demand of book titles and the availability of high priced book titles in the inventory. After the analysis, they realize that the high priced books are out of stock. They request the part number of the book titles that are priced greater than or equal to $50 so that they can order those books to ensure they have enough stock. In the analysis, they also realize that there would be an increasing demand for books on "Sailing." For information on the tables and column names in the OGCBooks database, refer to the table structure in Appendix A.

What You Do	How You Do It
1. List the books whose sale price is greater than or equal to $50.	a. In the **Editor** pane, type **`SELECT partnum, bktitle, slprice`** and then press **Enter.** b. Type **`FROM titles`** and press **Enter.** c. Type **`WHERE slprice >= 50`** d. On the **SQL Editor** toolbar, click **Execute** to execute the query. e. In the **Results** pane, observe that the book titles, whose sale price is greater than or equal to $50, are displayed.

2. List the details of the book that has "Sailing" as the book title.

a. In the `SELECT` clause, in the `WHERE` condition, hold down **Shift** and click before `slprice` to select the condition.

b. Type **`bktitle = 'Sailing'`**

c. On the **SQL Editor** toolbar, click **Execute** to execute the query.

d. In the **Results** pane, observe that the book with "Sailing" as the title is displayed.

e. Close the **Query Editor** window without saving the query.

TOPIC B

Compare Column Values

You now know how to list column values that are present in the table. Sometimes, the value itself may not be very useful. But when calculations are performed on the values and then compared with other information you have, the result can be more useful. In this topic, you will compare the column values to retrieve data based on information you have.

The information available in a database is enormous. When you retrieve data without specifying a condition, all the information from a table are displayed. From the information that is listed, the required information has to be searched manually. To avoid searching for information manually, you can include a condition and retrieve only the information that is required.

Comparison Operators

Comparison Operators

Definition:

Comparison operators are symbols used to compare two expressions or values. The output of a comparison operator is one of three values: TRUE, FALSE, or UNKNOWN. Comparison operators cannot be used with text, ntext, or image data types. In SQL, they are used in conditions.

Example: The Equal To Comparison Operator

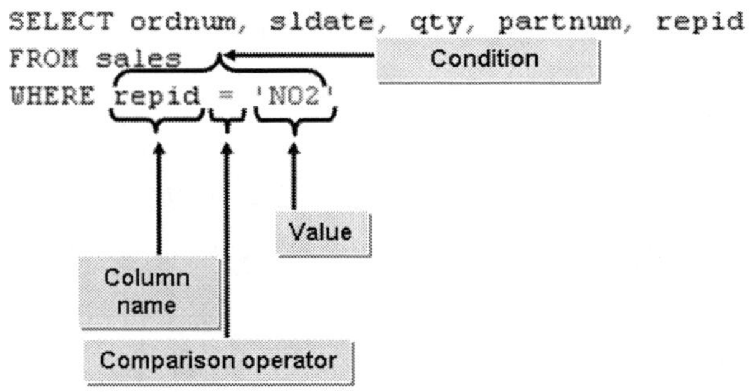
SELECT ordnum, sldate, qty, partnum, repid
FROM sales
WHERE repid = 'N02'
Condition
Value
Column name
Comparison operator

Comparison Operators and Their Description

There are nine comparison operators used in SQL.

Table 2-2: *Comparison Operators*

Comparison Operator	***Description***
=	Equal to
>	Greater than
<	Less than
>=	Greater than or equal to

Comparison Operator	Description
<=	Less than or equal to
<>	Not equal to
!=	Not equal to (not SQL-92 standard)
!<	Not less than (not SQL-92 standard)
!>	Not greater than (not SQL-92 standard)

Arithmetic Operators

Definition:

Arithmetic Operators

Arithmetic operators are symbols used to perform mathematical operations on numeric expressions. However, the plus (+) and minus (-) operators can also be used to perform arithmetic operations on datetime and smalldatetime values.

Arithmetic Operators Used in SQL

There are five arithmetic operators used in SQL.

Table 2-3: *Arithmetic Operators*

Arithmetic Operator	Description
+	Addition
-	Subtraction
*	Multiplication
/	Division
%	Modulo returns the integer remainder of a division.

Example: Using Arithmetic Operators in SQL

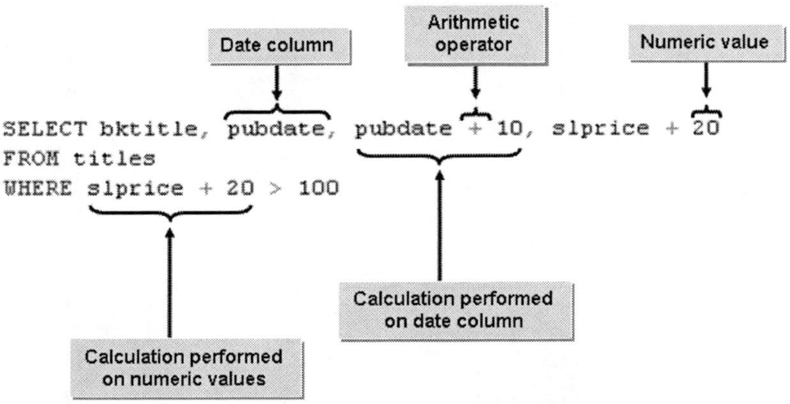
Date column
Arithmetic operator
Numeric value
SELECT bktitle, pubdate, pubdate + 10, slprice + 20
FROM titles
WHERE slprice + 20 > 100
Calculation performed on date column
Calculation performed on numeric values

Column Aliasing

Column Aliasing

Definition:

A *column alias* is a name assigned to a column heading in the output. A column alias can be assigned to any column in a table and is displayed in place of the default column heading. An alias makes it easier to interpret the contents of the column. The alias can contain any alphanumeric characters along with a few special characters.

Example: Using Column Alias in SQL

Calculation performed on column name

```
SELECT bktitle, slprice + 4 newslprice
FROM titles
WHERE slprice + 4 > 45
```

Alphanumeric character

Column alias displayed as column name

bktitle	newslprice
Clear Cupboards	53.95
Y2K, Why Worry?	49.00
The Sport of Hang Gliding	53.68
The Complete Football Reference	53.99
Woodworking Around the House	50.97
Minor Home Repairs Made Easy	49.95
More Home Repairs Made Easy	53.99

Default Column Headings

By default, the column name is displayed in the heading of the output. If the column does not have a column name because it is the result of a calculation, the heading “No column name” is displayed.

How to Compare Column Values

Procedure Reference: Compare Column Values

To compare the column values:

1. In the **Editor** pane, enter the `SELECT` clause followed by the column names and the calculated value that is required for the output.
2. If necessary, for clarity, include a column alias for any column name that has a calculated value.
3. Enter the `FROM` clause with the table name from where you need the output.
4. Enter the `WHERE` clause to include a condition.
    - Use comparison operators to compare the column value.
    - Use arithmetic and comparison operators to compare a calculated value with column values.
5. Click **Execute.**

ACTIVITY 2-2

Comparing Column Values

Before You Begin:

1. On the **Standard** toolbar, click **New Query** to open the **Query Editor** window.
2. On the **SQL Editor** toolbar, ensure that the OGCBooks database is selected from the **Available Databases** drop-down list.

Scenario:

Your boss comes up with an idea to promote the sales of the company by offering discounts for certain books. The plan is to provide 7% off on all books whose sale price is greater than $45 after the discount. You need to identify the book titles that will be included in the discount sale. For information on the tables and column names in the OGCBooks database, refer to the table structure in Appendix A.

What You Do	How You Do It
1. Display the titles of the books that have a sale price of $45 or above.	a. In the **Editor** pane, type **`SELECT bktitle, slprice`** and press **Enter**. b. Type **`FROM titles`** and press **Enter.** c. Type **`WHERE slprice >= 45`** d. On the **SQL Editor** toolbar, click **Execute** to execute the query. e. In the **Results** pane, observe that the list of books, whose sale price is greater than or equal to $45, are displayed.

2. Modify the query to display the books whose sale price is $45 and above after the discount. Also, display the sale price of the book after discount along with the original price of the book.

a. In the `SELECT` clause, click after `slprice` and type **`, slprice - slprice*0.07 discountprice`**

b. In the `WHERE` clause, click after `slprice` and type **`-slprice* 0.07`**

c. On the **SQL Editor** toolbar, click **Execute** to execute the query.

d. In the **Results** pane, observe that the list of books, whose sale price is greater than or equal to $45 after the discount along with their original saleprice, is displayed.

e. Close the **Query Editor** window without saving the query.

TOPIC C
Search Using Multiple Conditions

The search condition you provide to retrieve information determines the result obtained from the query. You are aware of simple conditions that display information. But the data in the database may sometimes be structured such that a simple condition would not be enough to display the output required. In this topic, you will use multiple search conditions to display the desired output.

Not all information can be retrieved using one simple condition. Let's say you have a database containing information about all the employees in a company. You need a list of employees in the marketing department who have been with the company for over five years, and who have not utilized their full vacation time. How would you do this using a simple condition? First, you could generate a list of all employees in the marketing department. Then, you could run another query to list the employees who have been with the company for over five years. Finally, you could get the list of employees who have not utilized their full vacation time. Then, you need to manually compare the output of the three lists and identify the employees who fall into this category. Or, you could accomplish all these tasks in one query using multiple search conditions.

Logical Operators

Logical Operators

Definition:

Logical operators are operators that test the truth of a condition. Logical operators, like comparison operators, return a value of either TRUE or FALSE. When more than one logical operator is used in a SQL statement, they are executed in an order that is previously determined. Parentheses can be used to change the order of evaluation.

Example: Using a Logical Operator

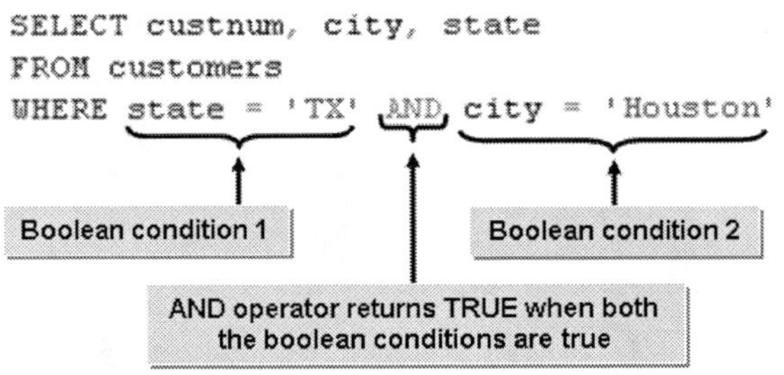
SELECT custnum, city, state
FROM customers
WHERE state = 'TX' AND city = 'Houston'
Boolean condition 1
Boolean condition 2
AND operator returns TRUE when both the boolean conditions are true

Example: Using Multiple Logical Operators

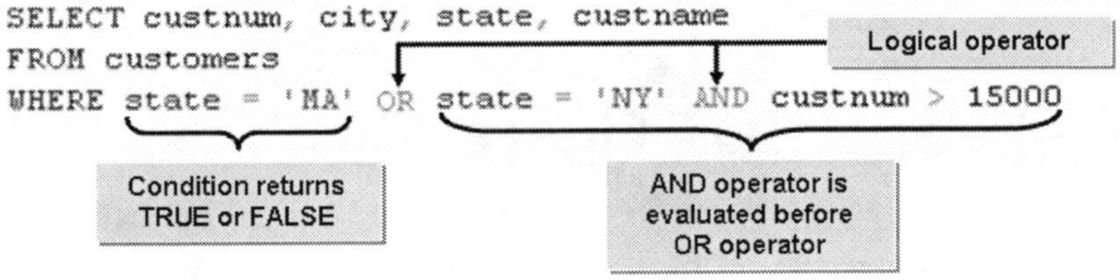
SELECT custnum, city, state, custname
FROM customers
WHERE state = 'MA' OR state = 'NY' AND custnum > 15000
Logical operator
Condition returns TRUE or FALSE
AND operator is evaluated before OR operator

Example: Using Multiple Logical Operators with Parentheses

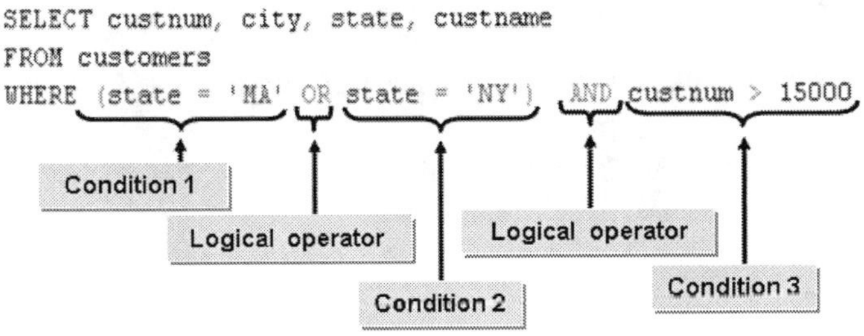
SELECT custnum, city, state, custname
FROM customers
WHERE (state = 'MA' OR state = 'NY') AND custnum > 15000
Condition 1
Logical operator
Condition 2
Logical operator
Condition 3

List of Logical Operators Used in SQL

There are 10 logical operators used in SQL.

Table 2-4: *Logical Operators*

Logical Operator	*Description*
AND	TRUE if both Boolean expressions are TRUE.
OR	TRUE if either Boolean expression is TRUE.
NOT	Reverses the value of any other Boolean operator.
BETWEEN	TRUE if the operand is within a range.
IN	TRUE if the operand is equal to one of a list of expressions.
LIKE	TRUE if the operand matches a pattern.
ALL	TRUE if all of a set of comparisons are TRUE.
ANY	TRUE if any one of a set of comparisons is TRUE.
EXISTS	TRUE if a subquery contains any rows.
SOME	TRUE if some of a set of comparisons are TRUE.

> Boolean is a type of an expression with two possible values, "true" and "false."

The AND, OR, and NOT Operators

The AND, OR, and NOT Operators

The AND, OR, and NOT operators are the most commonly used logical operators. The AND and OR operators are used to combine the result of two or more Boolean expressions. The AND operator returns TRUE when both the expressions are TRUE, while the OR operator returns TRUE when either of the expressions is TRUE. The NOT operator is used to negate a Boolean expression.

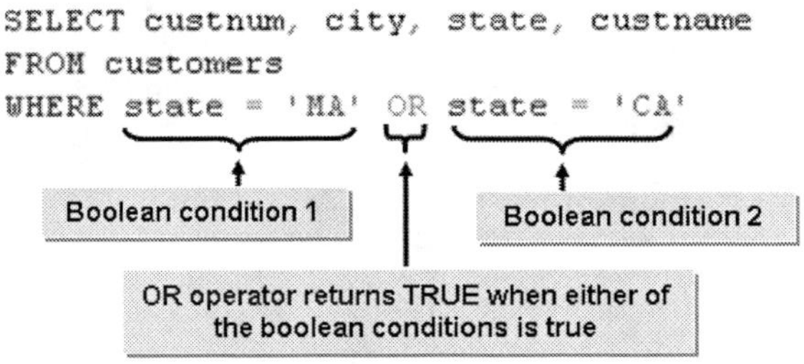

Figure 2-2: *The use of the OR operator in SQL.*

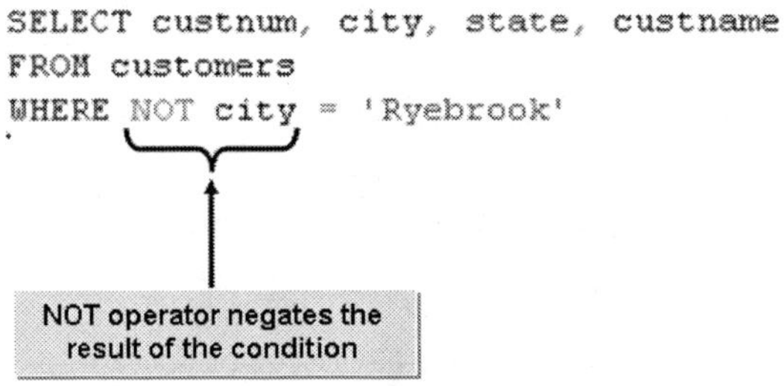

SELECT custnum, city, state, custname
FROM customers
WHERE state = 'MA' OR state = 'CA'
WHERE NOT city = 'Ryebrook'
NOT operator negates the result of the condition

Figure 2-3: *The use of the NOT operator in SQL.*

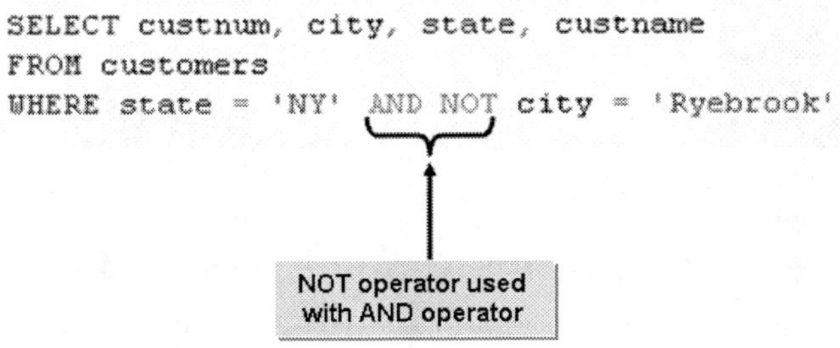
SELECT custnum, city, state, custname
FROM customers
WHERE state = 'NY' AND NOT city = 'Ryebrook'
NOT operator used with AND operator

Figure 2-4: *The use of the AND NOT operator in SQL.*

Syntax of Commonly Used Logical Operators

boolean_expression1 `AND` *boolean_expression2*

boolean_expression1 `OR` *boolean_expression2*

`[ NOT ]` *boolean_expression*

How to Search Using Multiple Conditions

Procedure Reference: Search Using Multiple Conditions

To search using multiple conditions:

1. In the **Editor** pane, enter the `SELECT` statement to list the required columns from a table.
2. Enter the first condition using the WHERE clause.
3. Include another condition along with the existing condition using a logical operator to narrow down the search.

   ```
   SELECT colname1, [colname2, ... ]
   FROM tablename
   WHERE condition1 logical_operator1 condition2 logical_operator2 ....
   ```
4. If necessary, include additional conditions using the logical operators.
   - If the operators used in the condition do not follow the operator hierarchy from left to right, then use parentheses.
   - If you need to list additional columns, then include them in the `SELECT` clause.
5. Execute the query.

ACTIVITY 2-3

Searching for Rows Using Multiple Conditions

Before You Begin:

1. On the **Standard** toolbar, click **New Query** to open the **Query Editor** window.
2. On the **SQL Editor** toolbar, ensure that the OGCBooks database is selected from the **Available Databases** drop-down list.

Scenario:

The sales manager gets information about a book exhibition that is to be conducted in Ryebrook, New York. He requires the list of customers in New York and the customers in the city of Ryebrook so that he can organize a stall in the book exhibition for the books published by OGC Books. The sales manager also decides to conduct a promotional sale in New York and Massachusetts. He wants to check if the representative with ID S01 is familiar with the customers in those states, so that he could be sent for the sale. For information on the tables and column names in the OGCBooks database, refer to the table structure in Appendix A.

What You Do	How You Do It
1. List all the customers who are from New York state.	a. In the **Editor** pane, type **`SELECT city, state, custname`** and press **Enter.** b. Type **`FROM customers`** and press **Enter.** c. Type **`WHERE state = 'NY'`** d. On the **SQL Editor** toolbar, click **Execute** to execute the query. e. In the **Results** pane, observe that a list containing customers from the New York state is displayed.

2. True or False? To list only the customers from the city of Ryebrook, add another condition along with the existing condition using the AND comparison operator.

✓ True

__ False

3. List all the customers who are either in the State of Massachusetts or New York.

a. In the `WHERE` clause, select the condition.

b. Type **`state = 'MA' OR state = 'NY'`**

c. On the **SQL Editor** toolbar, click **Execute** to execute the query.

d. In the **Results** pane, observe that a list of customers from the states of New York and Massachusetts is displayed

---

4. Do you use parentheses when more than two conditions are used in the SELECT statement?

a) No. Parentheses are not used.

✓ b) Parentheses are used when the operators used in conditions do not follow operator hierarchy.

c) Yes. Parentheses are always used.

d) Parentheses are used to enhance readability.

---

5. List the customers with the representative ID S01 who are either from Massachusetts or from New York.

a. In the `SELECT` clause, click after `custname` and type **`, repid`**

b. In the `WHERE` clause, click after `'NY'`, press the **Spacebar,** and type **`AND repid = 'S01'`**

c. On the **SQL Editor** toolbar, click **Execute** to execute the query.

d. In the **Results** pane, observe that a list of customers with representative ID S01, who are either from the state of Massachusetts or New York is displayed.

e. Close the **Query Editor** window without saving the query.

TOPIC D

Search for a Range of Values and Null Values

You know how to retrieve records present in the table based on conditions. There are times when you may need to retrieve information from the database based on a specified range. In this topic, you will search for records based on a range of values.

The output of a query depends on the condition that is used to retrieve the information. If there is a table that contains a list of book titles and their price, and you need only the list of books whose price range is between 40 and 50, then instead of using two conditions, you can use an operator to retrieve the records that fall in that range.

The BETWEEN..AND Operator

The BETWEEN..AND Operator

Definition:

The *BETWEEN..AND operator* is a logical operator that searches for an inclusive range of values. The start value of the range is entered after the `BETWEEN` keyword and the end value is entered after the `AND` keyword in the `WHERE` clause of a SQL statement. The logical operator `NOT` can be used to retrieve the records that fall outside the specified range.

Example: Search for a Range of Values

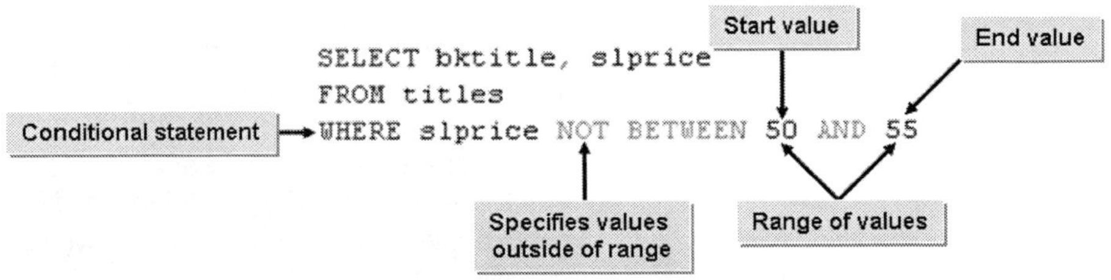

Syntax of the BETWEEN..AND Operator

```
expression1 [ NOT ] BETWEEN expression2 AND expression3
```

> The `BETWEEN..AND` operator is the equivalent of using >= and <= operators to frame a condition. Using the `BETWEEN..AND` operator rather than the mathematical symbols makes it easier to read and understand the code.

The IN Operator

Definition:

The IN Operator

The *IN operator* is a logical operator that checks whether a column value or expression matches a list of values. The IN operator is entered in the WHERE clause between the column name and the list of values to be matched. The list of values is entered within parentheses, separated by commas. If text is used in the list of values, it is enclosed within single quotes. The data type of the values in the list must match the data type of the column or expression.

Example: Search for a List of Values

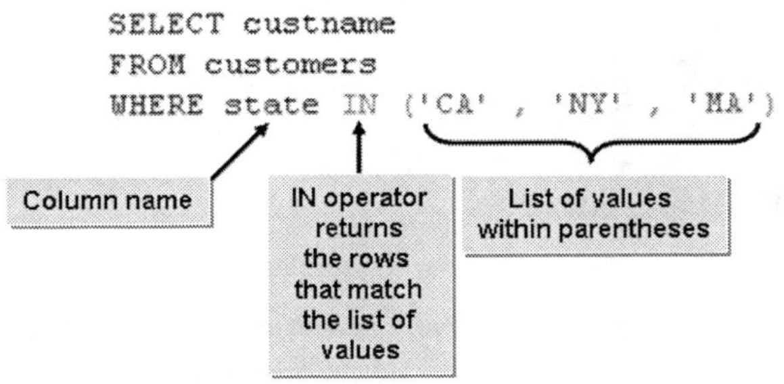
SELECT custname
FROM customers
WHERE state IN ('CA' , 'NY' , 'MA')
Column name
IN operator returns the rows that match the list of values
List of values within parentheses

Syntax of the IN Operator

expression [NOT] IN
(*expression [value1, value2, ...]*)

The NULL Value

Definition:

The NULL Value

NULL is a value that can be stored in a column when the value is either unknown or undefined. When the table information is viewed, the word "NULL" is displayed in the column that contains the null value. It is not the same as zero, blank, or a zero-length character string. When null values are compared, they will not be equal because the value of each NULL is unknown.

Example: Null Value Used in a Table

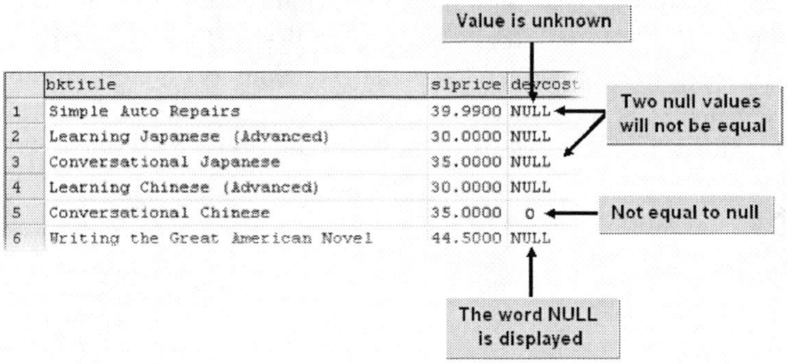

	bktitle	slprice	devcost
1	Simple Auto Repairs	39.9900	NULL
2	Learning Japanese (Advanced)	30.0000	NULL
3	Conversational Japanese	35.0000	NULL
4	Learning Chinese (Advanced)	30.0000	NULL
5	Conversational Chinese	35.0000	0
6	Writing the Great American Novel	44.5000	NULL

The IS NULL Clause

The IS NULL Clause

Definition:

The *IS NULL clause* is a clause that tests for a NULL value. The `IS NULL` clause is entered in a `WHERE` clause after the expression or column name to be tested. The `NOT` operator can be entered between the `IS` and `NULL` keywords to check for values that are not null.

Syntax for the IS NULL Clause

```
expression IS NULL

expression IS [NOT] NULL
```

Example: Search for Null Values

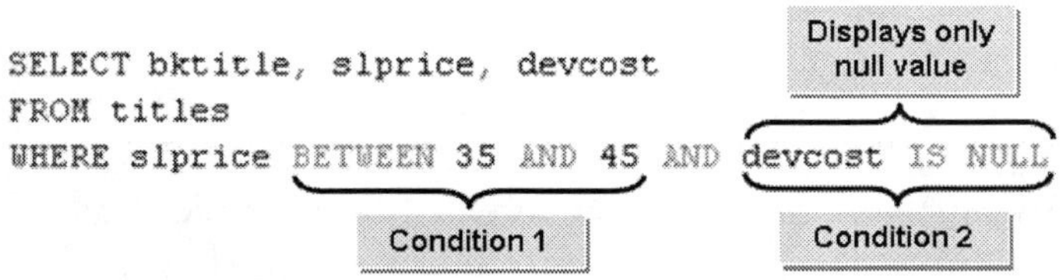

bktitle	slprice	devcost
Simple Auto Repairs	39.99	NULL
Conversational Japanese	35.00	NULL
Conversational Chinese	35.00	NULL
Writing the Great American Novel	44.50	NULL

Example: Search for Values That are Not Null

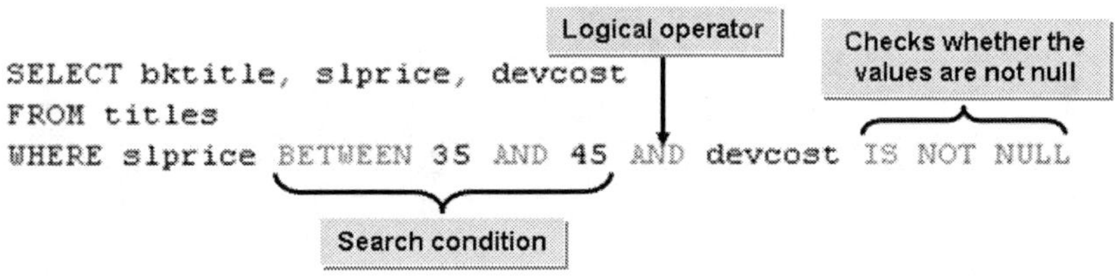
Logical operator
Checks whether the values are not null
SELECT bktitle, slprice, devcost
FROM titles
WHERE slprice BETWEEN 35 AND 45 AND devcost IS NOT NULL
Search condition

How to Search for a Range of Values and Null Values

Procedure Reference: Search for a Range of Values and Null Values

To search for a range of values and null values:

1. In the **Editor** pane, enter a `SELECT` statement to display the required column values from a specific table.
2. In the `WHERE` clause, use the `BETWEEN..AND` keywords to display the rows that satisfy the condition where a column name falls in a range of values.
3. If additional column values are required in the output, then place the mouse pointer after any column name listed in the `SELECT` clause and type the column name separated by a comma.
4. If necessary, add another condition to list all the rows with null values using the keywords `IS NULL` and execute the query.

   ```
   colname1 IS [NOT] NULL
   ```
5. If necessary, include the keyword `NOT` before the `NULL` keyword to display all the rows that have numeric values and execute the query.

ACTIVITY 2-4

Searching for a Range of Values and Null Values

Before You Begin:

1. On the **Standard** toolbar, click **New Query** to open the **Query Editor** window.
2. On the **SQL Editor** toolbar, ensure that the OGCBooks database is selected from the **Available Databases** drop-down list.

Scenario:

The manager of the sales department plans to implement a scheme that provides discounts to customers for books that are priced within a certain range. The manager also realizes that some of the books do not have the development cost, without which profit cannot be calculated. So he plans to identify the development cost before going ahead with the scheme. The list without the development cost was analyzed to determine why the cost was not recorded. The books with the development cost will be used to calculate the discount and also the profit obtained. For information on the tables and column names in the OGCBooks database, refer to the table structure in Appendix A.

What You Do	How You Do It
1. Generate a list of all the titles whose sale price is between $35 and $70.	a. In the **Editor** pane, type **`SELECT bktitle, slprice`** and press **Enter**. b. Type **`FROM titles`** and press **Enter.** c. Type **`WHERE slprice BETWEEN 35 AND 70`** d. On the **SQL Editor** toolbar, click **Execute** to execute the query. e. In the **Results** pane , observe that a list of book titles whose sales price is between $35 and $70 is displayed.

2. List the titles that do not have the development cost recorded.	a. In the `SELECT` clause, click after `slprice` and type **`, devcost`** b. In the *`WHERE`* clause, click after 70, press the **Spacebar,** and type **`AND devcost IS NULL`** c. On the **SQL Editor** toolbar, click **Execute** to execute the query. d. In the **Results** pane, observe that a list of book titles whose development cost are not recorded is displayed.
3. Modify the query to list the titles that have a numerical development cost.	a. In the `WHERE` clause click after `IS`, press the **Spacebar,** and type **`NOT`** b. On the **SQL Editor** toolbar, click **Execute** to execute the query. c. In the **Results** pane, observe that a list of titles that have a numerical development cost is displayed. d. Close the **Query Editor** window without saving the query.

TOPIC E

Retrieve Data Based on Patterns

You know how to search data using the comparison operators and arithmetic operators. If you do not know the exact value you are looking for but only know a certain part of the value, then you cannot use the comparison or arithmetic operators. In this topic, you will use another type of operator to search for specific combinations of characters.

When retrieving information from the database, you may not always know exactly what you are looking for. Suppose you have a customer database containing hundreds of customers and many of whose names are starting with the characters "Stan". Now, you would prefer to narrow down your search to retrieve the exact information you want. In such cases, you can search the database based on patterns to retrieve the information you need.

Wildcards

Wildcards

Definition:

A *wildcard* is a special character used in a search expression to represent other characters. Wildcards can be inserted anywhere within a search pattern to locate column values in records that contain a known sequence of characters without having to enter the entire string of characters, or when the entire set of characters is not known. There are four wildcard characters in SQL. Some wildcards substitute for a single character, while others substitute for an unlimited number of characters. More than one wildcard can be used in an expression.

Example: Using Wildcard to Search Characters

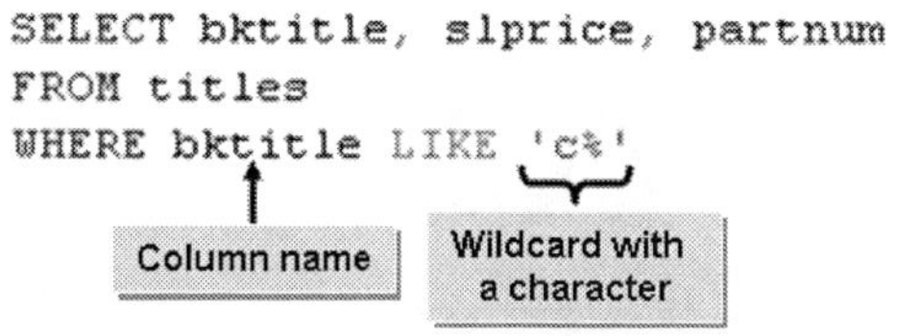
SELECT bktitle, slprice, partnum
FROM titles
WHERE bktitle LIKE 'c%'
Column name
Wildcard with a character

Example: Using More Than One Wildcard

```
SELECT bktitle, slprice, partnum
FROM titles
WHERE bktitle LIKE '%art%'
```

Wildcard used to search characters

Pattern

bktitle	slprice	partnum
Clear Cupboards	49.95	39843
Creating Toys in Wood	23.79	40521
Cross-stitching for Special Occasions	20.00	40522
Calligraphy	25.25	40569
Conversational Italian	35.00	40614
Conversational German	35.00	40624
Conversational French	35.00	40634
Conversational Japanese	35.00	40644

Output

The Four Wildcards Used in SQL

The four wildcard characters are used to match patterns in a SQL statement.

Table 2-5: *Wildcards Used in SQL*

Wildcard	*Meaning*
%	Any string of zero or more characters.
_	Any single character.
[ ]	Any single character within the specified range.
[^]	Any single character not within the specified range.

Pattern Matching

Definition:

Pattern matching is a method of searching for column values in a record whose exact value is not known, but which are known to contain a specific combination of text or numeric characters. The pattern being searched for can be a single character or a combination of characters, and may include one or more wildcards. Pattern matching tests whether the specified pattern exists anywhere within the value in the database. Pattern matching uses the `LIKE` operator followed by the pattern enclosed within single quotes. The characters used in the pattern are not case sensitive.

Pattern Matching

Example: Using Pattern Matching to Search Values

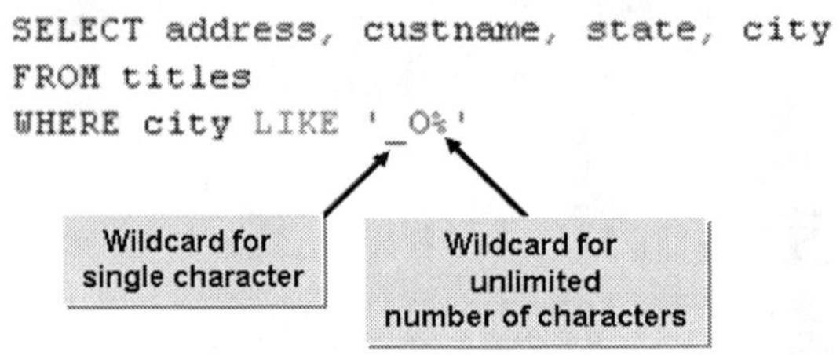

SELECT address, custname, state, city
FROM titles
WHERE city LIKE '_O%'
Wildcard for single character
Wildcard for unlimited number of characters

Syntax of the LIKE Operator

expression [NOT] LIKE *pattern*

The pattern should be enclosed within single quotes.

Operator Precedence

When multiple operators are used in a complex expression, operator precedence determines the sequence in which the operations are performed. A higher-level operator is evaluated before a lower-level operator. If the order of execution is not specified precisely using parentheses, the resulting output may not be correct.

Operators have precedence levels, based on which they are executed. Using parentheses, the order in which the operators are executed can be changed.

Operator Level	***Operator Precedence in Each Level***
1	+ (Positive), - (Negative), ~ (Bitwise NOT)
2	* (Multiply), / (Division), % (Modulo)
3	+ (Add), + (Concatenate), - (Subtract)
4	=, >, <, >=, <=, <>, !=, !>, !< (Comparison operators)
5	^ (Bitwise Exclusive OR), & (Bitwise AND), | (Bitwise OR)
6	NOT
7	AND
8	ALL, ANY, BETWEEN, IN, LIKE, OR, SOME
9	= (Assignment)

How to Retrieve Data Based on Patterns

Procedure Reference: Retrieve Data Based on Patterns

To retrieve data based on a pattern:

1. Identify the logic used to retrieve the data.
2. Enter the `SELECT` statement with column names that are required in the output and determine the table from where to retrieve this information.
3. Identify the condition that is required to retrieve the column values using wildcard and patterns.
4. Enter the condition using the `LIKE` keyword.

   ```
   WHERE colname LIKE pattern.
   ```
5. Execute the query.

ACTIVITY 2-5

Retrieving Data Based on Patterns

Before You Begin:

1. On the **Standard** toolbar, click **New Query** to open the **Query Editor** window.
2. In the **SQL Server Management Studio Express** window, on the **SQL Editor** toolbar, ensure that the OGCBooks database is selected from the **Available Databases** drop-down list.

Scenario:

A customer comes up to the salesperson and says that he wants a list of all the books that have information about art. After selecting the first book from the list of book titles, the customer wants to select the second book. He thinks the title of the book started with the characters A, M, or C. After seeing the list of books, he realizes that the search has to be extended for the book titles whose characters range from A to G. Another customer wants to know if his name and customer ID are still available in the database. He was a customer of this company a long time ago and does not remember his customer ID; he however remembers that it was a four-digit number, with the last digit being either 1 or 9. For information on the tables and column names in the OGCBooks database, refer to the table structure in Appendix A.

What You Do	How You Do It
1. Display the book titles that have the characters “art” in the title.	a. In the **Editor** pane, type **`SELECT bktitle, partnum, slprice`** and press **Enter.** b. Type **`FROM titles`** and press **Enter.** c. Type **`WHERE bktitle LIKE '%art%'`** d. On the **SQL Editor** toolbar, click **Execute** to execute the query. e. In the **Results** pane, observe that the books with the characters “art” in their titles are displayed.

2. Display the details of the books whose titles begin with A, M, or C.	a. Select the condition after `LIKE` b. Type `'[AMC]%'` c. On the **SQL Editor** toolbar, click **Execute** to execute the query. d. In the **Results** pane, observe that the books whose titles begin with A, M, or C are displayed.
3. Modify the query to display the details for the books whose titles begin with the characters from A to G.	a. Select the condition after the `LIKE` keyword. b. Type **`'[A-G]%'`** c. On the **SQL Editor** toolbar, click **Execute** to execute the query. d. In the **Results** pane, observe that the books whose titles begin with the characters from A to G are displayed. e. Close the **Query editor** window without saving the query.
4. List the customer details from the "customers" table for those who have a four-digit customer number.	a. On the **Standard** toolbar, click **New Query** to open the **Query Editor** window. b. From the **Available Databases** drop-down list, choose **OGCBooks.** c. Type **`SELECT custnum, custname, city FROM customers`** and press **Enter.** d. Type **`WHERE custnum LIKE '____'`** where the four underscores are included inside single quotes. e. On the **SQL Editor** toolbar, click **Execute** to execute the query. f. In the **Results** pane, observe that customers who have four-digit customer numbers are displayed.

5. Modify the query to list the customers with a four-digit customer number with the last digit being either 1 or 9.	a. Select `'____'` and type **`'___[19]'`** where the three underscores and [19] are included inside single quotes.
	b. On the **SQL Editor** toolbar, click **Execute** to execute the query.
	c. In the **Results**, pane, observe that customers who have four-digit customer numbers with the last digit being either 1 or 9, are displayed.
	d. Close the **Query editor** window without saving the query.

Lesson 2 Follow-up

In this lesson, you included search conditions in the `SELECT` statement to retrieve specific information from the database. These search conditions enabled you to narrow down the exact information that is required rather than manually searching for the information. You were able to search for a range of values, null values, and also search for patterns.

1. **Why do you use a condition in a query?**

   Answers will vary.

2. **What are the operators that you will use when you have more than one condition to be included in a query?**

   Answers will vary.

3 Working with Functions

Lesson Time: 50 minutes

Lesson Objectives:

In this lesson, you will use various functions based on the data types to perform calculations on data.

You will:

- Perform date calculations.
- Calculate data using aggregate functions.
- Manipulate string values in a query.

Introduction

In the previous lesson, you retrieved data from a database based on certain conditions. But you can do more than just display data that is in the database. You can perform calculations and other operations on the data and present the data in a format that is required. In this lesson, you will use various functions to perform calculations on the different data types to obtain a meaningful output from the database.

Suppose you have a database that contains all the employee information, and you need to identify the employees who have worked for over five years, along with their average salary. This information will not be readily available in the database. However, you can obtain this information by performing calculations on the data that is present in the database.

TOPIC A
Perform Date Calculations

The data present in the database can be of any data type. The date information is stored in the database in a particular format. But when this information is retrieved, you may want to view it in a different format. In this topic, you will use the date functions to display information and perform calculations on date information.

When time-related information is stored in the database, both date and time values can be stored. Suppose you need to calculate the age of the employees working in the company, or you require information about the employees who have joined in the last fifteen days. This information can be obtained by using date functions to perform the necessary calculations before displaying the output.

Functions

Functions

Definition:

A *function* is a piece of code with a specified name and optional parameters that operates as a single logical unit. The parameter can be a column name or a value. When more than one input parameter is supplied, the parameters are separated by commas. The function performs a designated action and returns a result.

Example: Functions in a SQL Statement

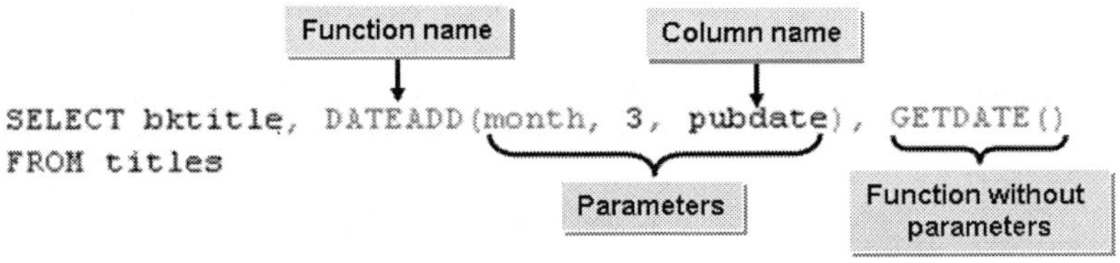
Function name
Column name
SELECT bktitle, DATEADD(month, 3, pubdate), GETDATE()
FROM titles
Parameters
Function without parameters

Types of Functions

There are three types of functions: rowset functions, which are used to reference tables in a SQL statement; aggregate functions, which operate on a collection of values but return a single value; and scalar functions, which operate on a single value and then return a single value. Scalar functions can be used in any valid expression. Functions can be classified as built-in functions, which cannot be modified by users, and user-defined functions, which can be created and modified by users.

Table 3-1: *Categories of Scalar Functions*

Category	***Description***
Configuration functions	Returns information about configuration settings.
Cursor functions	Returns information about the status of a cursor.
Date and time functions	Manipulates datetime and smalldatetime values.
Mathematical functions	Performs trigonometric, geometric, and other numeric operations.
Metadata functions	Returns information on the attributes of databases and database objects.
Security functions	Returns information about users and roles.
String functions	Manipulates char, varchar, nchar, nvarchar, binary, and varbinary values.
System functions	Operates or reports on various system level options and objects.
System statistical functions	Returns information regarding the performance of SQL Server.
Text and image functions	Manipulates text and image values.

Date Functions

Definition:

Date functions are used to perform calculations on date columns that contain a date and time input value and return a string, numeric, or date and time value. In date functions, datetime or smalldatetime values, if used, are enclosed within single quotes.

Date Functions

Example: Date Functions in a SQL Statement

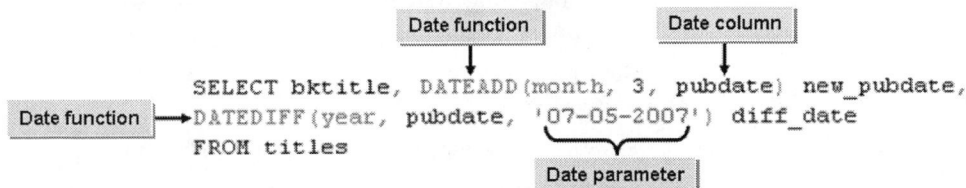

Date function (DATEADD) · Date column (pubdate) · Date function (DATEDIFF) · Date parameter ('07-05-2007')

```
SELECT bktitle, DATEADD(month, 3, pubdate) new_pubdate,
DATEDIFF(year, pubdate, '07-05-2007') diff_date
FROM titles
```

	bktitle	new_pubdate	diff_date
1	Clear Cupboards	2005-11-19 00:00:00	2
2	Y2K, Why Worry?	2006-04-01 00:00:00	1
3	Boating Safety	2006-08-18 00:00:00	1
4	Sailing	2006-08-03 00:00:00	1
5	The Sport of Windsurfing	2005-10-13 00:00:00	2
6	The Sport of Hang Gliding	2006-04-06 00:00:00	1
7	The Complete Football Reference	2005-11-03 00:00:00	2
8	How to Play Piano (Beginner)	2005-09-11 00:00:00	2
9	How to Play Piano (Intermediate)	2006-01-22 00:00:00	2
10	How to Play Piano (Advanced)	2006-03-01 00:00:00	2

Numeric values (diff_date) · Date and time values (new_pubdate)

> The `SET DATEFORMAT` statement can be used to set the order of the dateparts (month/day/year) for entering datetime or smalldatetime value.

List of Date Functions

The date functions are scalar functions that perform operations on date and time values.

Table 3-2: *Date Functions*

Function	*Description*
`DATEADD (`*`datepart, number, date`*`)`	Returns a new datetime value based on adding an interval to the specified date.
`DATEDIFF (`*`datepart, startdate, enddate`*`)`	Returns the number of date and time boundaries crossed between two specified dates.
`DATENAME (`*`datepart, date`*`)`	Returns a character string representing the specified datepart of the specified date.
`DATEPART (`*`datepart, date`*`)`	Returns an integer representing the specified datepart of the specified date.
`DAY (`*`date`*`)`	Returns an integer representing the day datepart of the specified date.
`GETDATE ( )`	Returns the current system date and time of the SQL Server in the format specified for datetime values.
`GETUTCDATE ( )`	Returns the datetime value representing the current UTC (Universal Time Coordinate or Greenwich Mean Time) time. The current UTC time is derived from the current local time and the time zone setting in the operating system of the computer on which SQL Server is running.
`MONTH (`*`date`*`)`	Returns an integer that represents the month part of a specified date.
`YEAR (`*`date`*`)`	Returns an integer that represents the year part of a specified date.

Datepart

Datepart is the word that specifies the part of the date to be returned, such as the year, month, day, and hour. Datepart is the input parameter entered in date functions. An abbreviation can be used in the date functions instead of entering datepart.

Abbreviations Used in Datepart

Following is the list of abbreviations of Datepart.

Table 3-3: *Datepart Abbreviations*

Datepart	Abbreviations
year	yy, yyyy
quarter	qq, q
month	mm, m
dayofyear	dy, y
day	dd, d
week	wk, ww
weekday	dw
hour	hh
minute	mi, n
second	ss, s
millisecond	ms

Using smalldatetime in Date Functions

The smalldatetime data type is accurate only to the minute. So, when a smalldatetime value is used with the date functions, the seconds and milliseconds returned are always zero.

How to Perform Date Calculations

Procedure Reference: Perform Date Calculations

To perform date calculations:

1. Identify the table and column names that contain date values to be used in calculations.
2. Enter the `SELECT` clause followed by the required columns.
3. Use the date functions to retrieve specific information from the date column.
4. If necessary, use other date functions to manipulate the columns that have date values.
5. Enter the `FROM` clause followed by the table name.
6. If necessary, enter the search condition for the query in the `WHERE` clause.
7. If necessary, use the date functions to form the conditions.
8. Execute the query.

ACTIVITY 3-1

Performing Date Calculations

Before You Begin:

1. On the **Standard** toolbar, click **New Query** to open a new **Query Editor** window.
2. On the **SQL Editor** toolbar, ensure that the OGCBooks database is selected from the **Available Databases** drop-down list.

Scenario:

The OGC Books publishing company is celebrating its 25th year in the market place. The management decides to release a "golden oldies" collection of the books released in the nineties. The details of the old books are available in the "obsolete_titles" table. The information required is a list of books that were released in the nineties, the year they were released, and the age of each book. For information on the tables and column names in the OGCBooks database, refer to the table structure in Appendix A.

What You Do	How You Do It
1. Identify the column name that contains the date information in the "obsolete_titles" table.	a. In the **Editor** pane, type **`SP_HELP obsolete_titles`** b. Execute the query. c. In the **Results** pane, observe that the "pubdate" row has `smalldatetime` as its data type. d. In the **Editor** pane, hold down **Shift,** and click before `SP_HELP` to select the command. e. Press **Delete** to clear the **Editor** pane.

2. **True or False? The DATEPART function can be used to extract the year from the published date of the book.**

✓ True

__ False

What You Do	How You Do It
3. Enter the query to list the details of the obsolete book titles, along with the year in which they were published and the age of the book.	a. In the **Editor** pane, type **`SELECT bktitle, DATEPART(YEAR, pubdate) year, DATEDIFF(YEAR, pubdate, GETDATE()) age`** and press **Enter.** b. Type **`FROM obsolete_titles`** and press **Enter.**

4. Enter the condition to select the books that were published only in the nineties and execute the query.

a. Type **`WHERE DATEPART(YEAR, pubdate) BETWEEN 1990 AND 1999`**

b. Execute the query.

c. In the **Results** pane, observe that the books that were published in the nineties are displayed.

d. Close the **Query Editor** window without saving the query.

TOPIC B

Calculate Data Using Aggregate Functions

In the previous topic, you used the date functions for calculations that involve date and time values. Calculations can be performed on other fields also. There are various functions used to perform calculations on the numerical data present in the database. In this topic, you will use the aggregate functions to perform calculations on numeric columns.

Databases can contain a large collection of unprocessed information. Sometimes, just extracting the information by itself may not be adequate for your needs. What may be more useful is to extract the data from the database, perform a calculation on it, and return a result of that calculation. For example, if you have an employee database and need to know, for a survey, the average age of the employees working in the organization, instead of manually going through the information in the database and using a calculator to find the average age, you can use SQL functions to perform the calculations and return the result.

Aggregate Functions

Aggregate Functions

Definition:

An *aggregate function* performs calculations on a set of values and returns a single value. The function is composed of two parts: a name that gives an indication of the calculation to be performed, followed by the values or references to the values, enclosed in parentheses. When the query with the aggregate function is executed, the result contains a single row with the summary information. Aggregate functions usually ignore null values.

Example: Using Aggregate Functions in SQL

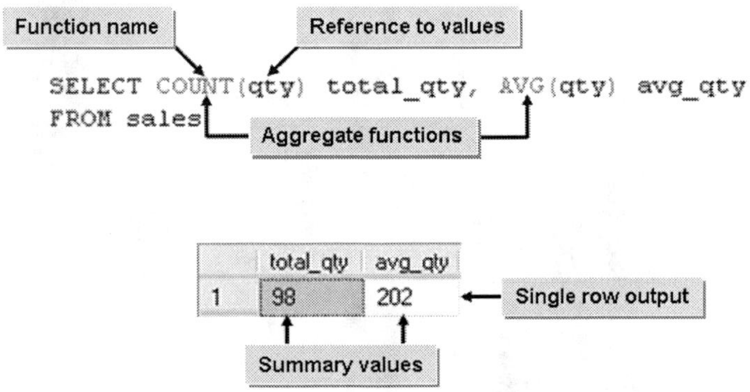

List of Aggregate Functions in SQL

All aggregate functions operate on a collection of values but return a single, summarizing value.

Table 3-4: *Aggregate Functions*

Aggregate Function	***Description***
`AVG(expression)`	Returns the average of the values in a column. The column can contain only numeric data.
`COUNT(expression)`, `COUNT(*)`	Returns a count of the values in a column (if you specify a column name as expression) or of all rows in a table or group (if you specify *). `COUNT(expression)` ignores null values, but `COUNT(*)` includes them in the count.
`MAX(expression)`	Returns the highest value in a column (last value alphabetically for text data types). Ignores null values.
`MIN(expression)`	Returns the lowest value in a column (first value alphabetically for text data types). Ignores null values.
`SUM(expression)`	Returns the total of values in a column. The column can contain only numeric data.

Keywords

Definition:

A *keyword* is a word that is reserved for defining, manipulating, and accessing data. When keywords are entered in the **Query Editor** window, they are displayed in color. Since a keyword has a predefined meaning in SQL, if used outside the predetermined context, it has to be enclosed within double quotes.

Keywords

> Keywords can also be used as identifiers or names of databases or database objects, such as tables, columns, and views.

Example: Using Keywords in SQL

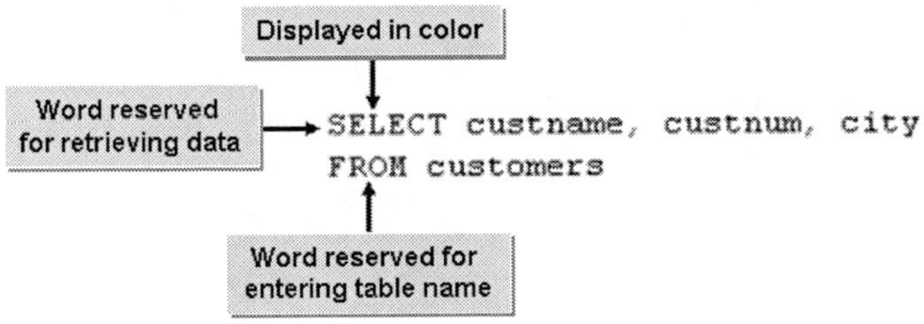

Non-Example: Using Keywords Outside the Context

```
SELECT custname, custnum, "from", city
FROM customers
```

Keyword used outside its predetermined context

The DISTINCT Keyword

The DISTINCT Keyword

Definition:

The *DISTINCT* keyword is used to eliminate duplicate values in a list of values. `DISTINCT` is an optional keyword that can be used in the `SELECT` statement to retrieve unique rows from the table. In the `SUM`, `AVG`, and `COUNT` functions, `DISTINCT` is used to eliminate duplicate values before performing calculations. If `DISTINCT` is used, it is used with column names and not with arithmetic expressions.

Example: DISTINCT Keyword Used in a SQL Statement

DISTINCT keyword

Column names

```
SELECT DISTINCT city, state
FROM customers
```

	city	state
1	Bellevue	WA
2	Buffalo	NY
3	Cambridge	MA
4	Cincinnati	OH
5	Denver	CO
6	East Har...	CT
7	Edina	MN
8	Fountain...	CA
9	Greensb...	NC
10	Houston	TX

No duplicate values

The COMPUTE Clause

The COMPUTE Clause

Definition:

A COMPUTE clause is a clause that generates totals that appear as additional summary columns at the end of a result set. When used with the keyword BY, it generates control breaks and subtotals in the result set. The COMPUTE clause contains the expression or column name on which the calculation is performed, and the expression or column name must appear in the SELECT statement. The COMPUTE and COMPUTE BY clauses can be used in the same query.

Example: Using the COMPUTE Clause

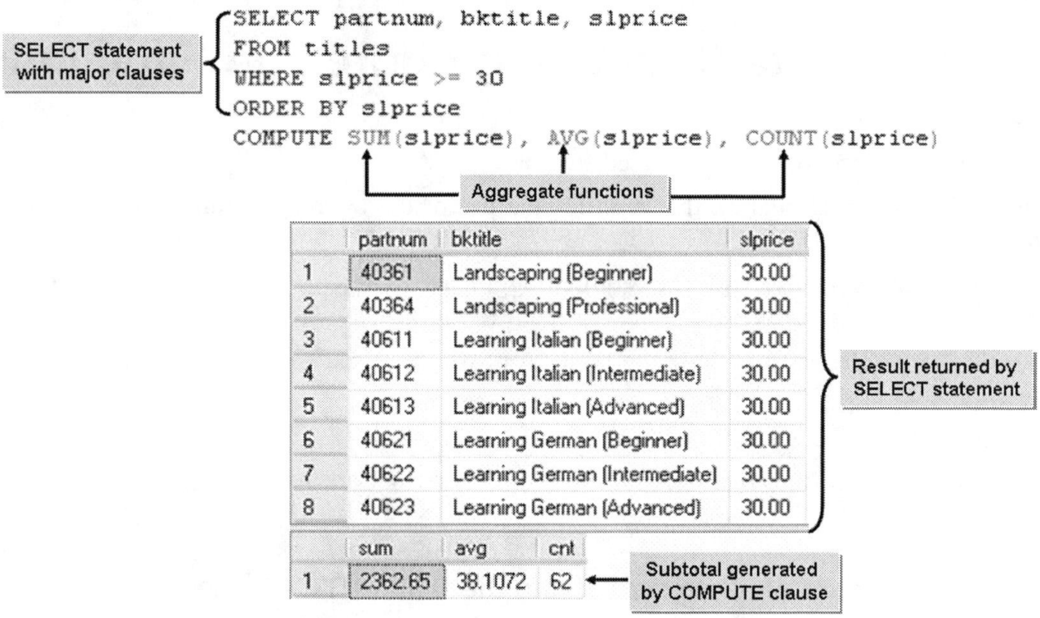


```
SELECT partnum, bktitle, slprice
FROM titles
WHERE slprice >= 30
ORDER BY slprice
COMPUTE SUM(slprice), AVG(slprice), COUNT(slprice)
```

	partnum	bktitle	slprice
1	40361	Landscaping (Beginner)	30.00
2	40364	Landscaping (Professional)	30.00
3	40611	Learning Italian (Beginner)	30.00
4	40612	Learning Italian (Intermediate)	30.00
5	40613	Learning Italian (Advanced)	30.00
6	40621	Learning German (Beginner)	30.00
7	40622	Learning German (Intermediate)	30.00
8	40623	Learning German (Advanced)	30.00

	sum	avg	cnt
1	2362.65	38.1072	62

Arguments in a COMPUTE Clause

The COMPUTE clause contains the following aggregate functions as arguments.

Table 3-5: *Aggregate Functions Used with the COMPUTE Clause*

Aggregate Function	***Result***
AVG	Returns the average of the values in the numeric expression.
COUNT	Returns the number of selected rows.
MAX	Returns the highest value in an expression.
MIN	Returns the lowest value in an expression.
STDEV	Returns the standard deviation for all values in an expression.
STDEVP	Returns the standard deviation for the population for all values in an expression.
SUM	Returns the total of the values in an expression.

Aggregate Function	Result
`VAR`	Returns the variance for all values in an expression.
`VARP`	Returns the variance for the population for all values in an expression.

Syntax of the COMPUTE Clause

COMPUTE {*Aggregate Function* (*expression*)} [,...*n*]

How to Calculate Data Using Aggregate Functions

Procedure Reference: Calculate Data

To calculate data and present a summarized output:

1. Identify the business situation that requires the use of the aggregate functions to generate summary values.
2. Enter the `SELECT` clause with the required aggregate function and the column name to display the result.
3. Enter the `FROM` clause to include the table from where to retrieve information.
4. Enter the condition in the `WHERE` clause to retrieve records used in the aggregate calculation mentioned in the `SELECT` clause.
5. If necessary, use the date functions or other operators that are required in the condition.
6. Execute the query.

Procedure Reference: Calculate Data Using the COMPUTE Clause

1. Identify the business situation that requires the use of the COMPUTE clause to generate summary values.
2. Enter the `SELECT` clause with the required column name to display in the result set.
3. Enter the condition in the `WHERE` clause to retrieve records.
4. If necessary, use the date functions or other operators that are required in the condition.
5. Enter the `COMPUTE` clause and the required aggregate functions with respective column names in the expressions.
6. Execute the query.
7. If necessary, save the query.

ACTIVITY 3-2

Calculating Data

Before You Begin:

1. On the **Standard** toolbar, click **New Query** to open a new **Query Editor** window.
2. On the **SQL Editor** toolbar, ensure that the OGCBooks database is selected from the **Available Databases** drop-down list.

Scenario:

The management wants to expand the OGC Books publishing company. The first step to accomplish this is to determine the revenue spent in the past and then estimate the investments to be made for the growth of the company. They've determined that sales figures for the year 2005 will be used for the analysis. The information required are the titles that were released, count of the titles that were released, the total development cost for all the books, and the average development cost for a title. A couple of titles do not have the development cost listed. For the analysis to be accurate, the management wants the list of these books so that they can request the development cost. The management also wants to have a complete list of all the book titles with their development cost and sale price in a result set and an additional set containing the count of the titles, the total development cost, and the average development cost. For information on the tables and column names in the OGCBooks database, refer to the table structure in Appendix A.

What You Do	How You Do It
1. List all the titles that were developed in the year 2005.	a. In the **Editor** pane, type **`SELECT bktitle FROM titles`** and press **Enter.**
	b. Type **`WHERE DATEPART(year, pubdate) = 2005`**
	c. Execute the query.
	d. In the **Results** pane, observe that all the books that were developed in the year 2005 are displayed.

2. Display the total number of titles released, the total cost of development for all the titles, and the average development cost for a title in the year 2005.	a. In the `SELECT` statement, double-click `bktitle` and press **Delete.** b. Type **`COUNT(bktitle) title_count, SUM(devcost) total_devcost, AVG(devcost) Average_cost`** c. Execute the query. d. In the **Results** pane, observe that the count of titles, the sum of the development cost, and the average cost of development for a title are displayed.
3. List the titles that have null values for the development cost.	a. In the `SELECT` statement, hold down **Shift**, and click before `COUNT` to select the column names along with their aliases. b. Press the **Spacebar** and type **`bktitle, devcost`** c. Click after `2005`, press the **Spacebar** and type **`AND devcost IS NULL`** to check if the development cost of the titles is null. d. Execute the query. e. In the **Results** pane, observe that two titles are displayed.
4. List the titles that were developed in the year 2005 with their development cost, sale price, and publication date.	a. In the `SELECT` statement, click after `devcost` and type **`, slprice, pubdate`** to display the columns in the result set. b. Select `AND devcost IS NULL` and press **Enter.**

5. Display the title count, the total development cost for all titles, and the average development cost for a title in the year 2005.

a. Type **`COMPUTE COUNT(bktitle), SUM(devcost), AVG(devcost)`** to display an additional summary column below the result set.

b. Execute the query.

c. In the **Results** pane, in the first result set, observe that the book titles along with their development cost, sale price, and publication date are displayed.

d. In the second result set, observe that the count of titles, the sum of development cost, and the average cost of development for a title are displayed.

e. Close the **Query Editor** window without saving the query.

TOPIC C
Manipulate String Values

In the previous topics, you used the date functions and aggregate functions. There are functions that can be used with other data type. These functions allow you to manipulate the column values and extract the information that is required. In this topic, you will use the string functions to effectively extract information from alphanumeric columns.

You display your output and find that values in two of the columns contain a lot of blank spaces. You're very sure you didn't put them there. How did they get there, and how do you get rid of them? This is one situation that calls for the use of string values. With string values, you can use functions to display the characters in the database based on your preferences.

Strings

Strings

Definition:

A *string* is a collection of characters that cannot be used in an arithmetic calculation. The char, varchar, and text data types are used to store strings. The characters can be uppercase or lowercase, numerals, and special characters such as the "at" sign (@), ampersand (&), and exclamation point (!) in any combination. String values used in expressions are enclosed within single quotes. When strings are compared, the case of the string is ignored.

Example: String Used in SQL

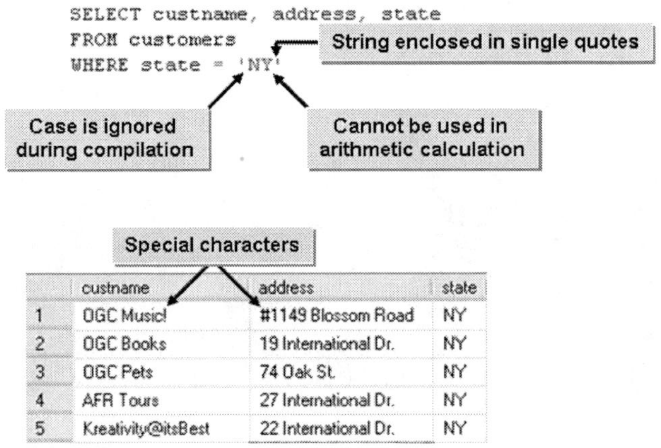

String Functions

String Functions

Definition:

String functions are functions that perform an operation on a string input value and return a string or a numeric value.

Example: String Function in a SQL Statement

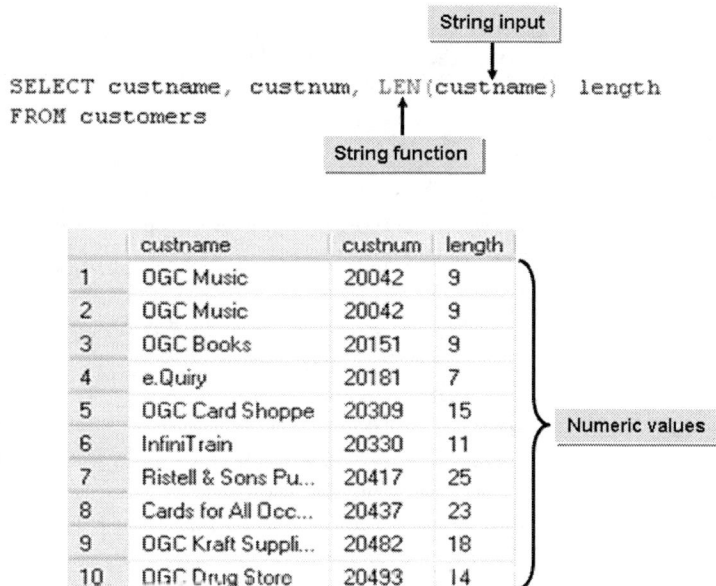

String input

```
SELECT custname, custnum, LEN(custname) length
FROM customers
```

String function

	custname	custnum	length
1	OGC Music	20042	9
2	OGC Music	20042	9
3	OGC Books	20151	9
4	e.Quiry	20181	7
5	OGC Card Shoppe	20309	15
6	InfiniTrain	20330	11
7	Ristell & Sons Pu...	20417	25
8	Cards for All Occ...	20437	23
9	OGC Kraft Suppli...	20482	18
10	OGC Drug Store	20493	14

Numeric values

String Functions Used in SQL

The string functions used in SQL are listed.

Table 3-6: *List of String Functions*

String Function	***Description***
`ASCII (`*`character_expression`*`)`	Returns the ASCII code value of the left most character of a character expression.
`CHAR (`*`integer_expression`*`)`	Converts an int ASCII code to a character.
`LEFT (`*`character_expression, integer_expression`*`)`	Returns the part of a character string starting at a specified number of characters from the left.
`RIGHT (`*`character_expression, integer_expression`*`)`	Returns the part of a character string starting at a specified number of *`integer_expression`* characters from the right.
`LEN (`*`string_expression`*`)`	Returns the number of characters, rather than the number of bytes, of the given string expression, excluding trailing blanks.
`STR (`*`float_expression`*` [, `*`length`*` [, `*`decimal`*` ] ] )`	Returns character data converted from numeric data.

String Function	Description
LOWER (*character_expression*)	Returns a character expression after converting uppercase character data to lowercase.
UPPER (*character_expression*)	Returns a character expression with lowercase character data converted to uppercase.
LTRIM (*character_expression*)	Returns a character expression after removing leading blanks.
RTRIM (*character_expression*)	Returns a character string after truncating all trailing blanks.
REPLACE ('*string_expression1*', '*string_expression2*', '*string_expression3*')	Replaces all occurrences of the second given string expression in the first string expression with a third expression.
REVERSE (*character_expression*)	Returns the reverse of a character expression.
REPLICATE (*character_expression*, *integer_expression*)	Repeats a character expression for a specified number of times.
SPACE (*integer_expression*)	Returns a string of repeated spaces.
STUFF (*character_expression*, *start*, *length*, *character_expression*)	Deletes a specified length of characters and inserts another set of characters at a specified starting point.
SUBSTRING (*expression*, *start*, *length*)	Returns part of a character, binary, text, or image expression.
UNICODE ('*ncharacter_expression*')	Returns the integer value, as defined by the Unicode standard, for the first character of the input expression.
NCHAR (*integer_expression*)	Returns the Unicode character with the given integer code, as defined by the Unicode standard.
SOUNDEX (*character_expression*)	Returns a four-character (SOUNDEX) code to evaluate the similarity of two strings.
DIFFERENCE (*character_expression*, *character_expression*)	Returns the difference between the SOUNDEX values of two character expressions as an integer.
QUOTENAME ('*character_string*' [, '*quote_character*'])	Returns a Unicode string with the delimiters added to make the input string a valid Microsoft® SQL Server™ delimited identifier.
PATINDEX ('*%pattern%*', *expression*)	Returns the starting position of the first occurrence of a pattern in a specified expression, or zeros if the pattern is not found, on all valid text and character data types.
CHARINDEX (*expression1*, *expression2* [, *start_location*])	Returns the starting position of the specified expression in a character string.

Case Conversion Functions

Definition:

Case conversion functions are functions that convert the case of a string. The `LOWER` function takes uppercase characters as the input and converts them to lowercase. The `UPPER` function takes lowercase characters as the input and converts them to uppercase. The input parameters provided for the case conversion functions can be a value or a column name.

Case Conversion Functions

Example: Case Conversion Functions in SQL

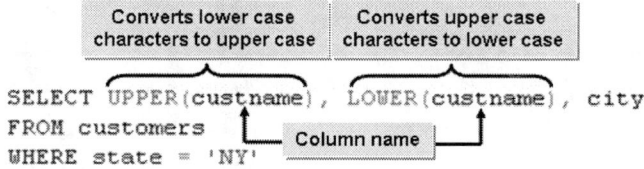

Converts lower case characters to upper case

Converts upper case characters to lower case

```
SELECT UPPER(custname), LOWER(custname), city
FROM customers
WHERE state = 'NY'
```

Column name

	(No column name)	(No column name)	city
1	OGC MUSIC	ogc music	Rochester
2	OGC BOOKS	ogc books	Ryebrook
3	OGC PETS	ogc pets	Buffalo
4	AFR TOURS	afr tours	Ryebrook
5	KREATIVITY@ITSBEST	kreativity@itsbest	Ryebrook

Output of the UPPER function

Output of the LOWER function

In the **Editor** pane, the case of the characters can be converted by selecting the words to be converted and pressing the key combinations **Ctrl+Shift+U** to convert the text to uppercase and **Ctrl+Shift+L** to convert the text to lowercase.

Leading and Trailing Spaces

Definition:

Leading and trailing spaces are spaces that are present in a column when the data stored in a column is less than the maximum number of characters that the column can contain. Spaces inserted before the value are called leading spaces, while those inserted at the end of the value are called trailing spaces.

Leading and Trailing Spaces

Example: Leading and Trailing Spaces in a Column Data

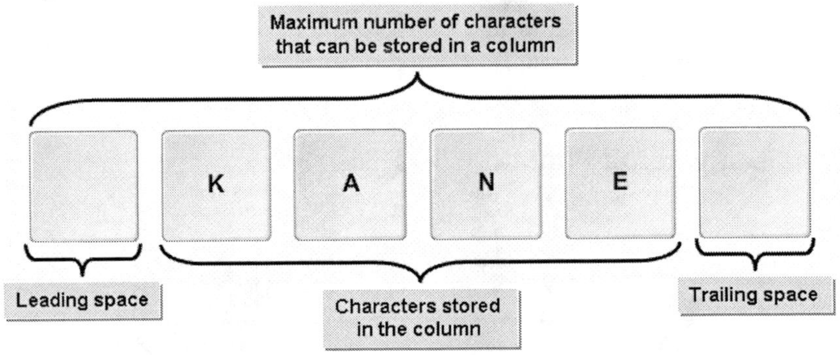

The Trim Function

The Trim Function

Definition:

A *trim function* removes the leading and trailing blank spaces that are part of a string. The LTRIM function removes the blank spaces before the value in a column and the RTRIM function removes the blank spaces after the value in a column. The trim function works only on string values.

Example: Trim Functions in a SQL Statement

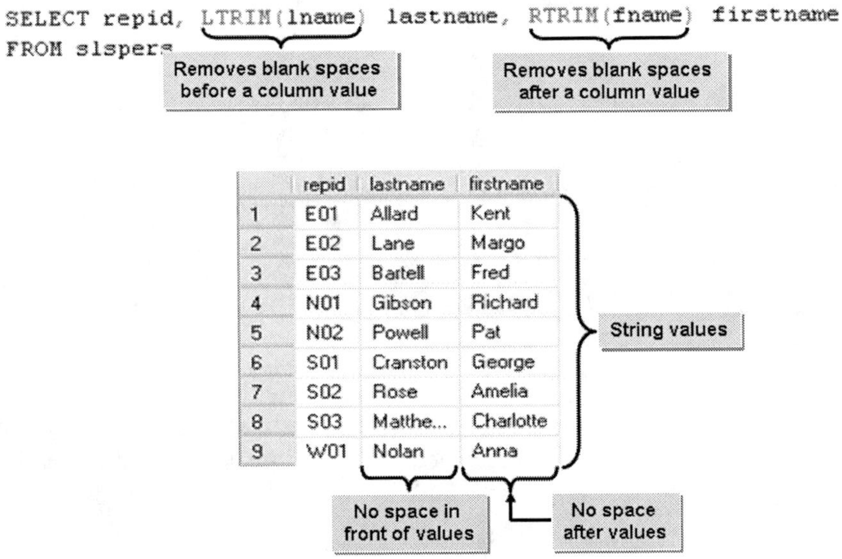

Character Extraction

Definition:

Character Extraction

Character extraction is the process of extracting specific characters from a string value. The extracted string is called a substring. Characters can be extracted from the beginning, end, or anywhere in the string.

Example: The Character Extraction Process

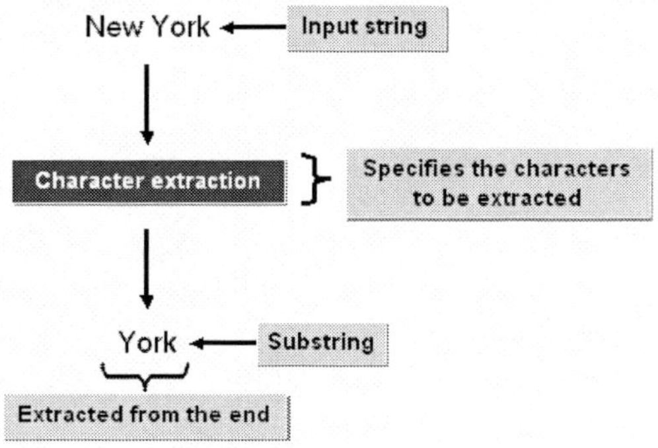

The SUBSTRING Function

Definition:

The SUBSTRING Function

SUBSTRING is a function used to extract characters from a given string. The `SUBSTRING` function takes three input parameters. The first parameter can be a character string, binary string, text, image, a column, or an expression that includes a column. Aggregate functions cannot be used as expressions. The second parameter is an integer that specifies where the substring begins. The third parameter is a positive integer that specifies the number of characters or bytes to be returned.

Example: Extracting Substrings

Column name

Integer specifies where the substring begins

```
SELECT custnum, SUBSTRING(custname, 5, 10) custname,
SUBSTRING('NEW YORK', 5, 4) statename
FROM customers
WHERE state = 'NY'
```

String value

Integer that specifies number of characters to be extracted

	custnum	custname	statename
1	20042	Music	YORK
2	20151	Books	YORK
3	20557	Pets	YORK
4	21133	Tours	YORK
5	21160	tivity@its	YORK

Extracted substrings

Data Types Supported by SUBSTRING

The output of this function can be character data if the expression is one of the supported character data types, binary data if the expression is one of the supported binary data types, or string if the expression is the same type as the given expression.

Concatenation

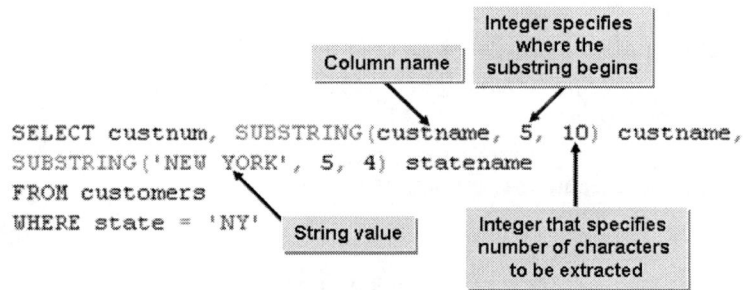

Concatenation

Definition:

Concatenation is the process of combining two string expressions into one string expression. If there are leading or trailing spaces in either of the expressions, then the other expression is appended following the spaces. The + (String Concatenation) operator is used to concatenate two expressions. Both expressions must be of the same data type, or one expression must be able to be implicitly converted to the data type of the other expression.

Example: Concatenation of Strings

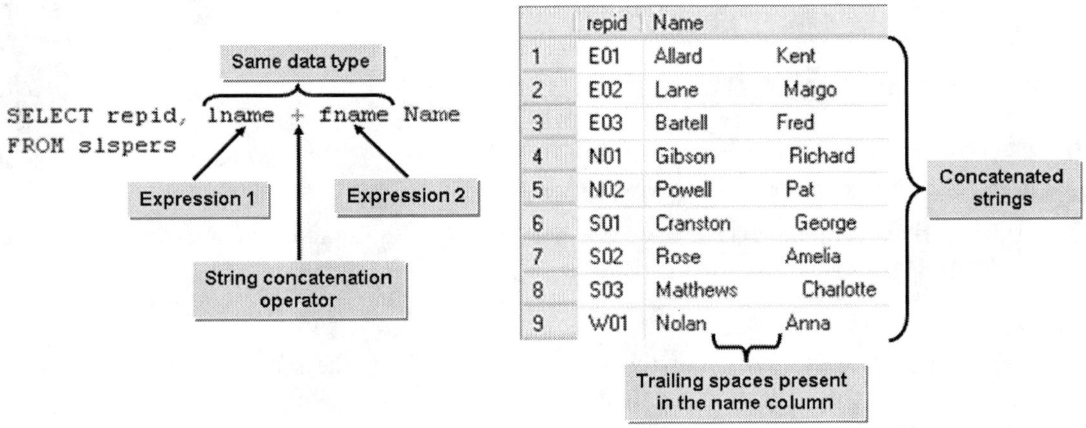

	repid	Name
1	E01	Allard Kent
2	E02	Lane Margo
3	E03	Bartell Fred
4	N01	Gibson Richard
5	N02	Powell Pat
6	S01	Cranston George
7	S02	Rose Amelia
8	S03	Matthews Charlotte
9	W01	Nolan Anna

String Concatenation Operator

```
expression + expression
```

Two or more character or binary strings, columns, or a combination of strings and column names form one expression. The expression used can be any of the data types in the character and binary data type category.

How to Manipulate String Values

Procedure Reference: Manipulate String Values

To manipulate string values:

1. Enter the `SELECT` clause followed by column names.
2. If multiple column values need to be displayed as a single column value, use the concatenation operator.
3. If necessary, enter a space or separators such as comma when concatenating columns.
4. Use the `RTRIM` and `LTRIM` functions to remove the leading and trailing spaces, respectively.
5. To display a column heading when using string functions, enter the column alias for the affected column.
6. Enter the `FROM` clause followed by the table name.
7. If necessary, enter a search condition.
8. Execute the query.

ACTIVITY 3-3

Manipulating String Values

Before You Begin:

1. On the **Standard** toolbar, click **New Query** to open a new **Query Editor** window.
2. On the **SQL Editor** toolbar, ensure that the OGCBooks database is selected from the **Available Databases** drop-down list.

Scenario:

After reviewing the performance of the sales representatives, the management decides to arrange a weekend trip as a mark of their appreciation. For booking tickets and fixing accommodation, the names of the representatives along with their representative IDs are required. To show their appreciation for the customers and to encourage them to purchase more titles, the management decides to send a "thank you" note to the customers along with some gifts. You have decided to list the required information. For information on the tables and column names in the OGCBooks database, refer to the table structure in Appendix A.

What You Do	How You Do It
1. List the first name and the last name for each representative from the "slspers" table.	a. In the **Editor** pane, type **`SELECT repid, RTRIM(fname)+' '+lname representative_name`** to display the representative ID along with the representative name. b. Press **Enter** and type **`FROM slspers`** to retrieve the information from the sales persons table. c. Execute the query. d. In the **Results** pane, observe that ten records are displayed.

2. List the customers and their addresses from the "customers" table.

a. In the **Editor** pane, select the entire query and press **Delete.**

b. Type **`SELECT custname, RTRIM(address)+','+RTRIM(city)`** to display the customer name, address, and city.

c. Press **Enter** and type **`+','+RTRIM(state) +','+RTRIM(zipcode)`**

d. Press the **Spacebar** and type **`Customer_address`** to create alias name for the customer address column.

e. Press **Enter** and type **`FROM customers`** to retrieve the information from the customers table.

f. Execute the query.

g. In the **Results** pane, observe that the list of customers and their addresses are displayed.

h. Close the **Query Editor** window without saving the query.

Lesson 3 Follow-up

In this lesson, you used functions on various data types to perform calculations. Using various functions, you can perform calculations on the information stored in the database to obtain the required output. The date functions are used when datetime and smalldatetime data types have to be manipulated. Aggregate functions are used to evaluate numeric values, and string functions are used to manipulate the string values stored in the database.

1. **Mention some instances where you used string functions.**

   Answers will vary.

2. **Which function is most commonly used in your project? Why?**

   Answers will vary.

4 Organizing Data

Lesson Time: 45 minutes

Lesson Objectives:

In this lesson, you will organize the data obtained from the query before it is displayed on the screen.

You will:

- Sort the query output to display the result in a specific order.
- Rank data.
- Group the data displayed in the output.
- Filter grouped data.
- Summarize grouped data.
- Use PIVOT and UNPIVOT operators.

Introduction

Retrieving data is the main function of the SQL query. Organizing the data helps you identify the information that you need instead of searching for it among the retrieved data. In this lesson, you will sort and group the data so that the required output is displayed.

In a database that has thousands of rows, only a few hundred rows may satisfy a given condition. If there is a need to identify the highest or lowest value from a list, you need to manually browse through the list. But if this list is sorted in either the ascending or the descending order, then it would be easier to identify the value you are looking for. Also, if you need information about the various categories that are available, instead of searching the list, you can group the list based on the categories.

TOPIC A
Sort Data

When you retrieve a large collection of data and want to search for a specific row, you will have to look through the entire list of contents. But, if the list is sorted in a particular order, then it becomes easy to identify the information. In this topic, you will sort the output based on one or more column names.

In a database that contains a large collection of information, finding the required information involves using a search condition. For example, in a banking database, if you list the transactions for one day, a few thousand rows will be listed. From this list, if the transactions made by any one customer have to be identified, sorting the list by the customer name would list all transactions of each customer in order.

Sorting

Sorting

Definition:

Sorting is a method of arranging column values displayed in the output in either the ascending or the descending order. The ascending sort arranges the values from the lowest to the highest, while the descending sort arranges values from the highest to the lowest. Multiple levels of sorting can be performed with a given set of rows.

Example: Sorting in Ascending Order

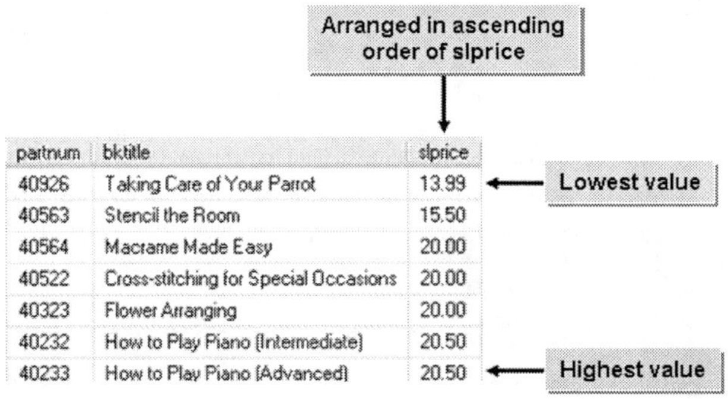

partnum	bktitle	slprice
40926	Taking Care of Your Parrot	13.99
40563	Stencil the Room	15.50
40564	Macrame Made Easy	20.00
40522	Cross-stitching for Special Occasions	20.00
40323	Flower Arranging	20.00
40232	How to Play Piano (Intermediate)	20.50
40233	How to Play Piano (Advanced)	20.50

Example: Sorting in Descending Order

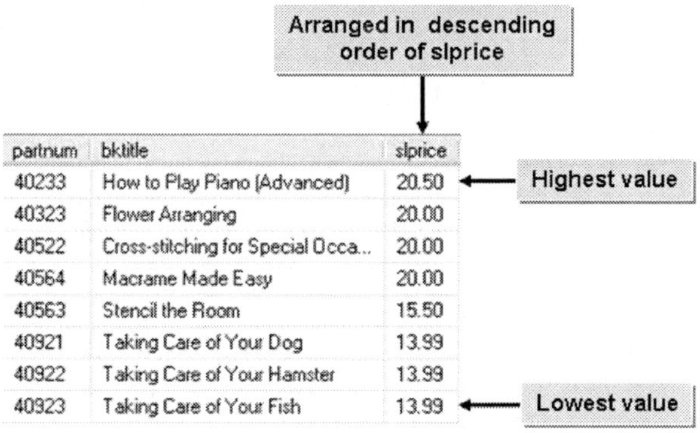

partnum	bktitle	slprice
40233	How to Play Piano (Advanced)	20.50
40323	Flower Arranging	20.00
40522	Cross-stitching for Special Occa...	20.00
40564	Macrame Made Easy	20.00
40563	Stencil the Room	15.50
40921	Taking Care of Your Dog	13.99
40922	Taking Care of Your Hamster	13.99
40923	Taking Care of Your Fish	13.99

The ORDER BY Clause

Definition:

ORDER BY is a clause used to display rows in a specified sort order. The `ORDER BY` clause is followed by the column name, and then the optional keyword `ASC` for ascending order or `DESC` for descending order. When neither keyword is specified, the `ORDER BY` clause sorts the rows in the ascending order. Multiple levels of sorting can be performed by specifying the column names, one after the other, separating them with commas. The null values present in the columns are treated as the lowest value. The `ORDER BY` clause, when used, is entered at the end of the SQL statement.

The ORDER BY Clause

Example: Using the ORDER BY Clause

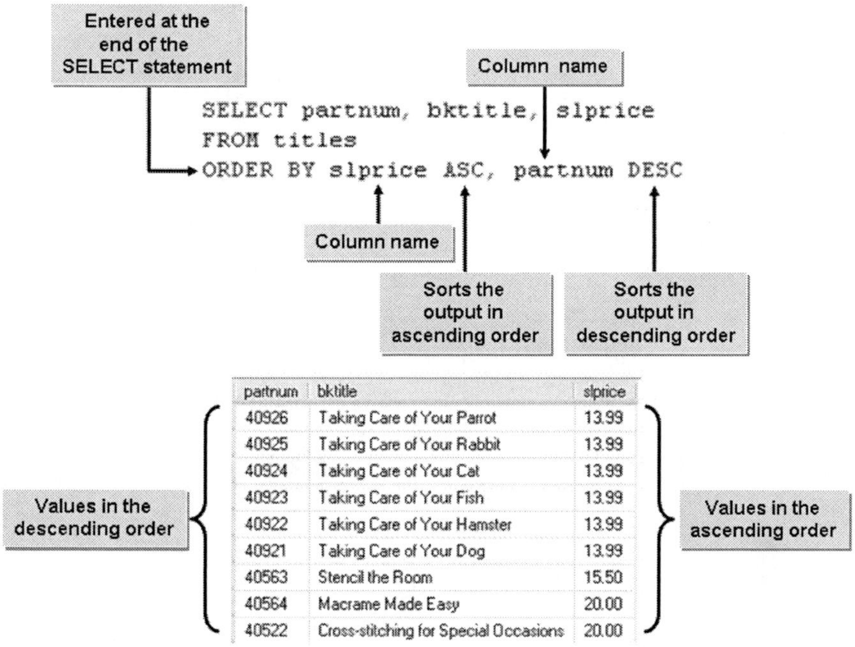


```
SELECT partnum, bktitle, slprice
FROM titles
ORDER BY slprice ASC, partnum DESC
```

partnum	bktitle	slprice
40926	Taking Care of Your Parrot	13.99
40925	Taking Care of Your Rabbit	13.99
40924	Taking Care of Your Cat	13.99
40923	Taking Care of Your Fish	13.99
40922	Taking Care of Your Hamster	13.99
40921	Taking Care of Your Dog	13.99
40563	Stencil the Room	15.50
40564	Macrame Made Easy	20.00
40522	Cross-stitching for Special Occasions	20.00

Syntax of the ORDER BY clause

```
[ ORDER BY [colname1, colname2,...] [ ASC | DESC ]  ]
```

Columns that contain ntext, text, or image data types cannot be sorted.

How to Sort Data

Procedure Reference: Sort Data

To sort data:

1. Enter the SELECT statement followed by the names of the columns required in the result.
2. If necessary, enter a column alias to make the output meaningful.
3. Enter the FROM clause followed by the table name.
4. To sort the columns, enter the ORDER BY clause followed by the column name or a calculated value.
5. If necessary, include the DESC keyword after the column name to sort the records in the descending order.
6. If necessary, include a secondary sort column in the ORDER BY clause separated by a comma.
7. If necessary, include a search condition.
8. Execute the query.

ACTIVITY 4-1

Sorting Data

Before You Begin:

1. On the **Standard** toolbar, click **New Query** to open the **Query Editor** window.
2. On the **SQL Editor** toolbar, ensure that the OGCBooks database is selected from the **Available Databases** drop-down list.

Scenario:

The management in a book publishing company has set up a team to analyze the profit and loss of the company. They require information about the book titles and their prices, listing books from the most expensive to the least expensive. They also want the number of books that need to be sold to break even. For information on the tables and column names in the OGCBooks database, refer to the table structure in Appendix A.

What You Do	How You Do It
1. List the book titles along with their sale price for all the book titles in the "titles" table. Sort this list in the descending order of the sale price and in the ascending order of the book titles.	a. Enter the `SELECT` statement to display the book title and sale price from the "titles" table and press **Enter.** b. Type **`ORDER BY slprice DESC, bktitle`** to sort the records in the descending order of the sale price and then in the ascending order of the book title. *See Code Sample 1.* c. Execute the query. d. In the **Results** pane, observe that the book titles are displayed with their sale price displayed in the descending order. e. Close the **Query Editor** window without saving the query.

Code Sample 1

```
SELECT bktitle, slprice FROM titles
ORDER BY slprice DESC, bktitle
```

2. **True or False? From the "titles" table, to calculate break even, you need to divide the development cost by the sale price of the book.**

✓ True

__ False

3. Display the information about the books and the number of copies to be sold to break even for the books that have the development cost listed.

a. On the **Standard** toolbar, click **New Query** to open the **Query Editor** window.

b. On the **SQL Editor** toolbar, from the **Available Databases** drop-down list, select **OGCBooks.**

c. In the **Editor** pane, enter the `SELECT` statement followed by the book title, development cost, sale price, and the break even sales number for each book.

See Code Sample 2.

d. Press the **Spacebar,** type **`copies_to_break_even`** as the alias name for the break even column, and press **Enter.**

e. Enter the `FROM` clause followed by the "titles" table name.

f. Enter the `WHERE` clause to filter the rows that do not have development cost listed.

g. Specify the `ORDER BY` clause to sort the output on the break even column value.

See Code Sample 3.

h. Execute the query.

i. In the **Results** pane, observe that the book titles along with their development cost, sale price, and the number of copies to be sold to break even are displayed.

j. Close the **Query Editor** window without saving the query.

Code Sample 2

```
SELECT bktitle, devcost, slprice, devcost/slprice
```

Code Sample 3

```
SELECT bktitle, devcost, slprice, devcost/slprice copies_to_break_even
FROM titles
WHERE devcost IS NOT NULL
ORDER BY devcost/slprice
```

TOPIC B

Rank Data

In the previous topic, you sorted data. Generally, data with the same values are sorted in a specific order. You may wish to rank them based on predefined criteria. In this topic, you will rank data.

For a survey on how many people have a Masters degree in an organization, you would like to identify and group the information available in the table based on their area of specialization. After grouping, you may wish to rank the people in each group based on their grade. This result can be obtained by ranking the grouped data.

The Ranking Functions

The Ranking Functions

Definition:

A ranking function is a function that sequentially numbers the rows in a result set based on the partitioning and ordering of the rows. Depending on the ranking function used in the query, some of the rows might get the same rank value as other rows. A ranking function is always followed by the `OVER` clause, which determines the partitioning and ordering of the rows before a ranking function is applied. The `OVER` clause is supported by the `PARTITION BY` clause, which determines how the rows are grouped for ranking, and the `ORDER BY` clause, which determines the order of the rows within each partition.

Example:

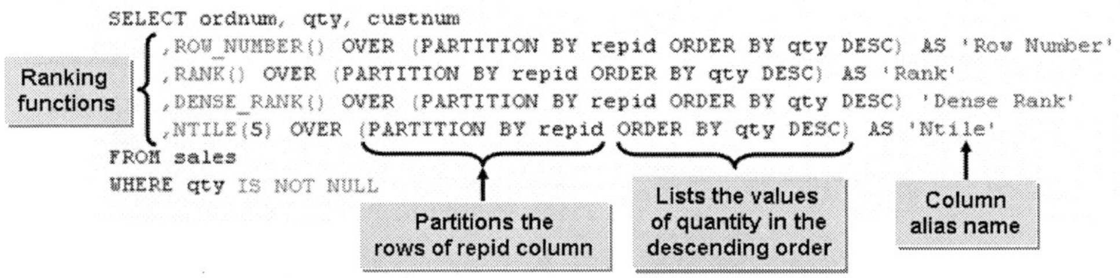
SELECT ordnum, qty, custnum
,ROW_NUMBER() OVER (PARTITION BY repid ORDER BY qty DESC) AS 'Row Number'
,RANK() OVER (PARTITION BY repid ORDER BY qty DESC) AS 'Rank'
,DENSE_RANK() OVER (PARTITION BY repid ORDER BY qty DESC) 'Dense Rank'
,NTILE(5) OVER (PARTITION BY repid ORDER BY qty DESC) AS 'Ntile'
FROM sales
WHERE qty IS NOT NULL
Ranking functions
Partitions the rows of repid column
Lists the values of quantity in the descending order
Column alias name

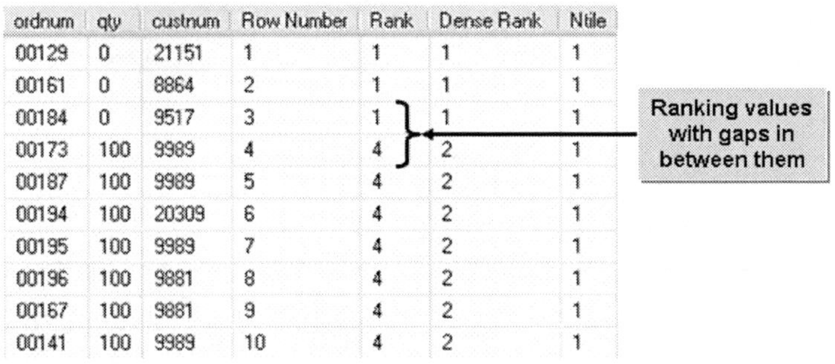

ordnum	qty	custnum	Row Number	Rank	Dense Rank	Ntile
00129	0	21151	1	1	1	1
00161	0	8864	2	1	1	1
00184	0	9517	3	1	1	1
00173	100	9989	4	4	2	1
00187	100	9989	5	4	2	1
00194	100	20309	6	4	2	1
00195	100	9989	7	4	2	1
00196	100	9881	8	4	2	1
00167	100	9881	9	4	2	1
00141	100	9989	10	4	2	1

Ranking values with gaps in between them

Syntax of a Ranking Function

The syntax of a ranking function is:

```
Ranking Function () OVER ([PARTITION BY value_expression,...[n]] ORDER BY
<column>[ASC | DESC][,...[n]])
```

The RANK Function

Definition:

The RANK Function

The *RANK* function is a ranking function that returns a ranking value for each row in a result set. The rank values returned by the RANK function are not continuous. If two or more rows of a table have the same value, they will be assigned the same rank value. In such a case, the ranking value gets increased as specified by the ORDER BY clause.

Example: RANK Function Used in a SQL Statement

```
SELECT  repid, qty, custnum
,RANK() OVER (PARTITION BY repid ORDER BY qty DESC) AS 'Rank'
FROM sales
WHERE qty > 300
```

Partitions the rows of repid column

Lists the values of quantity in the descending order

Column alias name

repid	qty	custnum	Rank
E01	500	9517	1
E01	500	9517	1
E01	350	9517	3
E01	330	9881	4
E01	330	9881	4
E01	330	9881	4
E02	500	20181	1
E02	500	20181	1
N01	400	20503	1
N01	370	20503	2

Ranking values with gaps in between them

Syntax of the RANK Function

The syntax of the RANK functions is:

```
RANK () OVER ( [< partition_by_clause>] <order_by_clause>)
```

The DENSE_RANK Function

Definition:

The DENSE_RANK Function

The *DENSE_RANK* is a ranking function that performs the task similar to that of the RANK function, but it does not produce gaps in the rank values. Instead, this function consecutively ranks each unique ORDER BY value.

Example: DENSE_RANK Function Used in a SQL Statement

```
SELECT repid, qty, custnum
,DENSE_RANK() OVER (PARTITION BY repid ORDER BY qty DESC) AS 'Dense rank'
FROM sales
```

Partitions the rows of repid column

Lists the values of quantity in the descending order

Column alias name

repid	qty	custnum	Dense rank
E01	500	9517	1
E01	500	9517	1
E01	350	9517	2
E01	330	9881	3
E01	330	9881	3
E01	330	9881	3
E02	500	20181	1
E02	500	20181	1
N01	400	20503	1
N01	370	20503	2

Consecutive rank values

Syntax of the DENSE_RANK Function

```
DENSE_RANK () OVER ( [< partition_by_clause>] <order_by_clause>)
```

The ROW_NUMBER Function

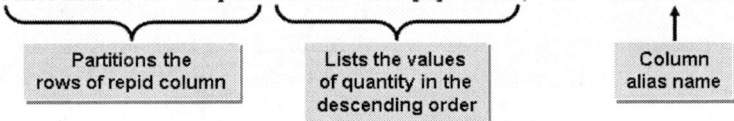

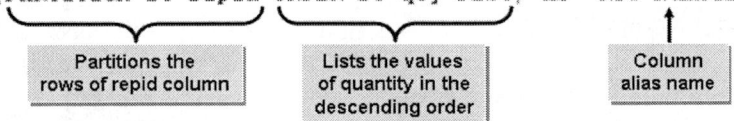

The ROW_NUMBER Function

Definition:

The *ROW_NUMBER* is a ranking function that uses an ORDER BY clause and a unique partition value to return a result set, which consists of sequential numbers for each row set. The row number() is subject to change according to the result.

Example: ROW_NUMBER Function Used in a SQL Statement

```
SELECT repid, qty, custnum
, ROW_NUMBER() OVER (PARTITION BY repid ORDER BY qty DESC) AS 'Row Number'
FROM sales
```

Partitions the rows of repid column

Lists the values of quantity in the descending order

Column alias name

	repid	qty	custnum	Row Number
1	E01	500	9517	1
2	E01	500	9517	2
3	E01	350	9517	3
4	E01	330	9881	4
5	E01	330	9881	5
6	E01	330	9881	6
7	E01	250	9517	7
8	E01	250	9881	8
9	E01	200	9881	9
10	E01	200	9517	10

Sequential numbering of each row

Syntax of the ROW_NUMBER function

```
ROW_NUMBER () OVER ( [< partition_by_clause>] <order_by_clause>)
```

The NTILE Function

The NTILE Function

Definition:

The NTILE is a ranking function that divides the rows in each partition of a result set into a specified number of groups based on a given value and ranks them according to the partition. The NTILE function contains an integer expression as its main argument, which specifies the number of groups into which each partition will be divided. The rows in the result set will be divided evenly among the partitions, but when the number of rows in the result set does not divide exactly into the number of partitions, the rows are distributed in such a way that the larger groups appear first in the result set.

Example: NTILE Function Used in a SQL Statement

```
SELECT repid, qty, custnum
,NTILE(5) OVER (PARTITION BY repid ORDER BY qty DESC) AS 'Ntile'
FROM sales
```

Partitions the rows of repid column

Lists the values of quantity in the descending order

Column alias name

	repid	qty	custnum	Ntile
1	E01	500	9517	1
2	E01	500	9517	1
3	E01	350	9517	2
4	E01	330	9881	2
5	E01	330	9881	3
6	E01	330	9881	4
7	E02	500	20181	1
8	E02	500	20181	2
9	N01	400	20503	1
10	N01	370	20503	2

Ranks after grouping and partition

Syntax of the NTILE function

```
NTILE (integer_expression) OVER ( [< partition_by_clause>]
<order_by_clause>)
```

How to Rank Data

Procedure Reference: Rank Data

To rank data:

1. Enter the `SELECT` statement followed by the columns that will be displayed in the result set.
2. Enter the desired rank function followed by the `OVER` clause.
3. If necessary, add more rank functions.
4. Enter the `FROM` clause followed by the table name.
5. Enter the `WHERE` clause followed by the search condition in order to make the result more specific.
6. Execute the query.

ACTIVITY 4-2

Ranking Data

Before You Begin:

1. On the **Standard** toolbar, click **New Query** to open the **Query Editor** window.
2. On the **SQL Editor** toolbar, ensure that the OGCBooks database is selected from the **Available Databases** drop-down list.

Scenario:

The management of the OGC Books publishing company has set up a team to analyze the performance of the sales representatives based on their sales quantity during the year 2006. Even though, they have a report containing the total sales quantity for the year 2006, they want to list the representatives based on the sales made by them during that year. You would like to use ranking functions to list the representatives based on the quantity of books they sold in 2006. For information on the tables and column names in the OGCBooks database, refer to the table structure in Appendix A.

What You Do	How You Do It

1. Which ranking function is used to partition the rows into a specified number of groups?

a) ROW_NUMBER ()

b) DENSE_RANK ()

✓ c) NTILE ()

d) RANK ()

2. List the representative IDs along with the quantity of books sold by each representative and the customer number. Rank the representative IDs based on the quantity of books sold by each representative.

a. Enter the `SELECT` statement followed by the representative IDs, the quantity of books sold by each representative, and the customer number.

b. Type **`, RANK () OVER(PARTITION BY repid ORDER BY qty DESC) AS 'Rank'`** to assign rank values for each row in the result after partitioning the representative IDs and listing the sales quantity in the descending order.

See Code Sample 1.

c. Press **Enter** and type **`, DENSE_RANK () OVER(PARTITION BY repid ORDER BY qty DESC) AS 'Dense Rank'`** to assign consecutive rank values for each row in the result after partitioning the representative IDs and listing the sales quantity in the descending order.

See Code Sample 2.

Code Sample 1

```
SELECT repid, qty, custnum
, RANK () OVER(PARTITION BY repid ORDER BY qty DESC) AS 'Rank'
```

Code Sample 2

```
SELECT repid, qty, custnum
, RANK () OVER(PARTITION BY repid ORDER BY qty DESC)
, DENSE_RANK () OVER(PARTITION BY repid ORDER BY qty DESC) AS 'Dense Rank'
```

3. Divide the rows into five groups and rank the representative IDs based on the quantity of books sold by each representative and display the row number for each row.

a. Press **Enter** and type **, NTILE (5) OVER(PARTITION BY repid ORDER BY qty DESC) AS 'Ntile'** to specify five groups of rows, and rank each row after partitioning the result set based on the representative IDs and listing the sales quantity in the descending order.

See Code Sample 3.

b. Press **Enter** and type **, ROW_NUMBER () OVER(PARTITION BY repid ORDER BY qty DESC) AS 'Row Number'** to display the row number for each row after partitioning the result set based on the representative IDs and listing the sales quantity in the descending order.

See Code Sample 4.

Code Sample 3

```
SELECT repid, qty, custnum
, RANK () OVER(PARTITION BY repid ORDER BY qty DESC) AS 'Rank'
, DENSE_RANK () OVER(PARTITION BY repid ORDER BY qty DESC) AS 'Dense Rank'
, NTILE (5) OVER(PARTITION BY repid ORDER BY qty DESC) AS 'Ntile'
```

Code Sample 4

```
SELECT repid, qty, custnum
, RANK () OVER(PARTITION BY repid ORDER BY qty DESC) AS 'RANK'
, DENSE_RANK () OVER(PARTITION BY repid ORDER BY qty DESC) AS 'Dense Rank'
, NTILE (5) OVER(PARTITION BY repid ORDER BY qty DESC) AS 'Ntile'
, ROW_NUMBER () OVER(PARTITION BY repid ORDER BY qty DESC) AS 'Row Number'
```

4. Rank all the representatives based on their sales quantity listed in the "sales" table for the year 2006.

a. Press **Enter** and type the `FROM` clause followed by the "sales" table.

b. Press **Enter** and enter the `WHERE` clause to display the quantity that is not null and the sales date for the year 2006.

See Code Sample 5.

c. Execute the query.

d. In the **Results** pane, observe that different ranks are given for the representative IDs based on the quantity of sales they made during the year 2006.

e. Close the **Query Editor** window without saving the query.

Code Sample 5

```
SELECT repid, qty, custnum
, RANK () OVER(PARTITION BY repid ORDER BY qty DESC)
, DENSE_RANK () OVER(PARTITION BY repid ORDER BY qty DESC) AS 'Dense Rank'
, NTILE (5) OVER(PARTITION BY repid ORDER BY qty DESC) AS 'Ntile'
, ROW_NUMBER () OVER(PARTITION BY repid ORDER BY qty DESC) AS 'Row Number'
FROM sales
WHERE qty IS NOT NULL AND DATEPART(year, sldate) = 2006
```

TOPIC C

Group Data

In the previous topic, you ranked the output of a query. In addition to ranking the output, you can also group data based on categories. In this topic, you will group data that belong to the same category.

People use organizers to keep track of their daily activities. If you need information about the activities performed on a particular date, then all you need to do is turn to the page for the particular date in the organizer for the information. Similarly, when the information in the database is large, to access the information you need, you can categorize the information so that the information required is displayed and you don't need to search manually for it.

Groups

Groups

Definition:

A *Group* is a collection of two or more records combined into one unit based on one or more columns. The records present in each group are listed together in the output. The groups are not sorted in any order, but the records within the group are sorted in the ascending order.

Example: Grouping Records

partnum	bktitle	devcost	slprice	pubdate
40121	Boating Safety	15421.81	36.50	2006-05-18 00:00:00
40122	Sailing	9932.96	29.15	2006-05-03 00:00:00
40123	The Sport of Windsurfing	12798.32	38.50	2005-07-13 00:00:00
40124	The Sport of Hang Gliding	15421.81	49.68	2006-01-06 00:00:00

Input Table

Collection of records based on one or more columns

partnum	bktitle	devcost	slprice	pubdate
40121	Boating Safety	15421.81	36.50	2006-05-18 00:00:00
40124	The Sport of Hang Gliding	15421.81	49.68	2006-01-06 00:00:00
40123	The Sport of Windsurfing	12798.32	38.50	2005-07-13 00:00:00
40122	Sailing	9932.96	29.15	2006-05-03 00:00:00

Records of each group are listed here

Output Table

The GROUP BY Clause

The GROUP BY Clause

Definition:

GROUP BY is a clause used to group two or more rows displayed in the output based on one or more columns. The `GROUP BY` clause is followed by a column or a non-aggregate expression that references a column. A `GROUP BY` clause must comply with certain specifications when written as part of a `SELECT` statement.

Example: Using Aggregate Functions When Grouping Records

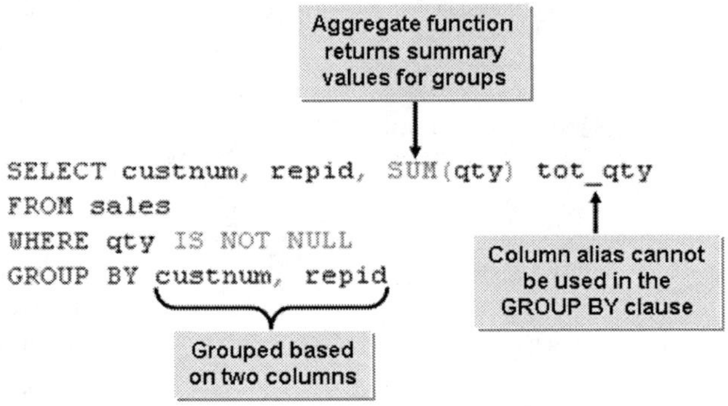
Aggregate function returns summary values for groups
SELECT custnum, repid, SUM(qty) tot_qty
FROM sales
WHERE qty IS NOT NULL
GROUP BY custnum, repid
Column alias cannot be used in the GROUP BY clause
Grouped based on two columns

Example: Using Non-Aggregate List When Grouping Records

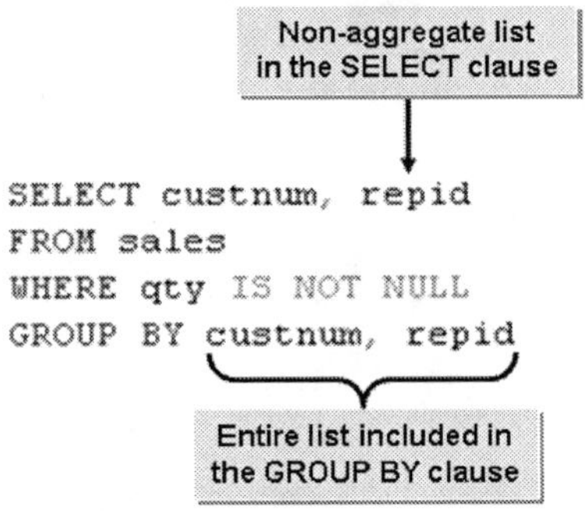
Non-aggregate list in the SELECT clause
SELECT custnum, repid
FROM sales
WHERE qty IS NOT NULL
GROUP BY custnum, repid
Entire list included in the GROUP BY clause

Syntax of the GROUP BY Clause

`[ GROUP BY [`*`group_by_expression1, group_by_expression2,.`*`] ]`

Using the ORDER BY Clause in Groups

If the `ORDER BY` clause is not specified, groups returned by the `GROUP BY` clause are not in any particular order. To retrieve a sorted output, include the `ORDER BY` clause in the query.

Specifications for Using a Group By Clause

A GROUP BY clause must comply with certain specifications when written as part of a SELECT statement.

Specification	***Description***
Multilevel groups	Multilevel groups can be formed by entering the columns separated by a comma. The number of levels is limited by the size of the data stored in the column, aggregate columns, and aggregate values involved in the query.

Specification	Description
Aggregate functions	If aggregate functions are entered in the SELECT clause, after the groups are formed, the summary values are calculated.
Non-aggregate list	When a non-aggregate list of values is entered in the SELECT clause, the entire list of values should be included in the GROUP BY list.
Null values	If the column on which the group is formed contains null values, the null values are put in a single group.
Column alias	The column alias used in the SELECT clause cannot be used to specify a grouping column.

How to Group Data

Procedure Reference: Group Data

To group data:

1. Identify the rows that you need to group based on the column.
2. Enter the `SELECT` clause followed by the appropriate columns that are required in the output.
3. If required, in the `SELECT` clause, include an aggregate function.
4. Enter the `FROM` clause followed by the table name.
5. If necessary, enter the `WHERE` clause to search for a condition.
6. Enter the `GROUP BY` clause to group the output based on a non-aggregate column.

   ```
   GROUP BY colname1 [, aggregate_colname, ...]
   ```
7. If necessary, include the `ORDER BY` clause to arrange the output in either the ascending or the descending order.
8. Execute the query.

ACTIVITY 4-3

Grouping Data

Before You Begin:

1. On the **Standard** toolbar, click **New Query** to open the **Query Editor** window.
2. On the **SQL Editor** toolbar, ensure that the OGCBooks database is selected from the **Available Databases** drop-down list.

Scenario:

You are given the task of collecting information about the total sales made by each representative, to each customer, over a period of six months. This information will be used to evaluate the representative's performance and also to set targets. For information on the tables and column names in the OGCBooks database, refer to the table structure in Appendix A.

What You Do	How You Do It

1. Which of the following columns need to be listed in the SELECT statement in order to list the total quantity of books sold by the representative to a customer?

a) AVG(qty), custnum, repid

b) custnum, repid

✓ c) SUM(qty) total_qty, custnum, repid

d) SUM(qty)/COUNT(qty), custnum, repid

2. True or False? The columns, used in the SELECT clause, that do not have the aggregate function need to be used in the GROUP BY clause.

✓ True

__ False

3. Enter a query to display the total sales by a representative to each customer during the first six months of the year 2006. Also, eliminate the rows that have the null value as the quantity.

a. Enter the `SELECT` statement followed by the `FROM` clause to retrieve the customer number, representative ID, and sum of the quantity from the "sales" table.

b. Enter the `WHERE` clause to retrieve only the records that fall within the first six months of the year 2006.

See Code Sample 1.

c. Type **`AND qty IS NOT NULL`** to filter the rows that have columns with null values in the "qty" column and press **Enter.**

Code Sample 1

```
SELECT custnum, repid, SUM(qty) total_sales
FROM sales
WHERE DATEPART(year, sldate) = 2006 AND DATEPART(month, sldate) BETWEEN 1 AND 6
```

4. Group the columns based on the customer number and then by the representative ID.

a. Type **`GROUP BY custnum, repid`** to group the output based on the customer number and then by the representative ID.

b. Execute the query.

c. In the **Results** pane, observe that total sales by each representative in the first six months of the year 2006 is displayed.

d. Close the **Query Editor** window without saving the query.

TOPIC D
Filter Grouped Data

In the previous topic, you grouped data. When data is grouped, all the rows that form a part of that group are listed together. You can further filter the grouped data by adding conditions. In this topic, you will filter records from grouped data using aggregate functions.

Suppose you have a table that contains the sales details of representatives in an organization. If you want to list only the representatives who have made sales of $2000 or more for a particular month, you need to group the records based on the representatives and calculate their total sales. Then, you can identify the representatives whose total sales is greater than $2000.

The HAVING Clause

The HAVING Clause

Definition:

HAVING is a clause used to specify a search condition for a group or an aggregate value. The `HAVING` clause is generally used with the `GROUP BY` clause. After the data has been grouped and aggregated, the conditions in the `HAVING` clause are applied. When the `GROUP BY` clause is not used, the `HAVING` clause behaves like a `WHERE` clause.

Example: Using the HAVING Clause with the GROUP BY Clause

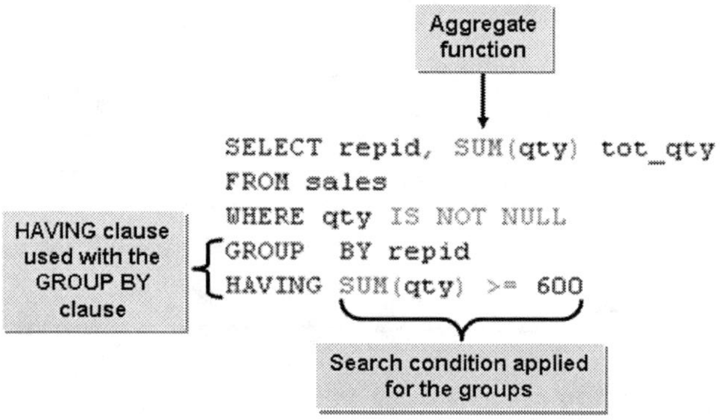
Aggregate function
SELECT repid, SUM(qty) tot_qty
FROM sales
WHERE qty IS NOT NULL
GROUP BY repid
HAVING SUM(qty) >= 600
HAVING clause used with the GROUP BY clause
Search condition applied for the groups

Example: Using the HAVING Clause Without the GROUP BY Clause

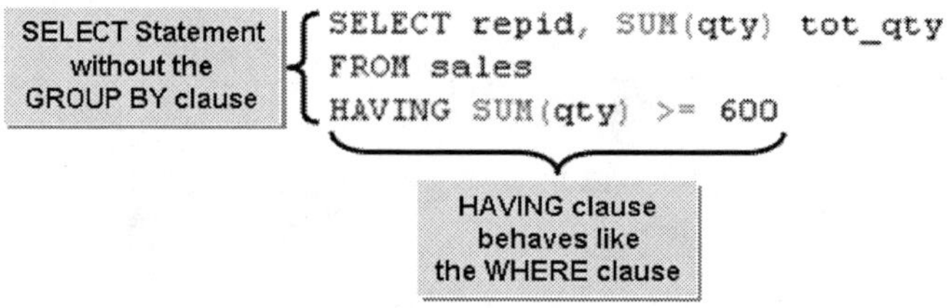
SELECT Statement without the GROUP BY clause
SELECT repid, SUM(qty) tot_qty
FROM sales
HAVING SUM(qty) >= 600
HAVING clause behaves like the WHERE clause

Compare the HAVING and WHERE Clause

The `HAVING` clause is similar to the `WHERE` clause, but applies only to the group as a whole, whereas the `WHERE` clause applies to individual rows. A query can contain both the `HAVING` and the `WHERE` clauses. The `WHERE` clause checks the condition for the `SELECT` clause. Similarly, the `HAVING` clause sets conditions on the `GROUP BY` clause. The search condition in the `WHERE` clause is applied before the grouping operation, and the search condition in the `HAVING` clause is applied after the grouping operation. The `HAVING` clause is similar to the `WHERE` clause, but can contain aggregate functions. The `HAVING` clause can reference any of the items that appear in the select list.

How to Filter Grouped Data

Procedure Reference: Filter Grouped Data

To filter the grouped data:

1. Identify the aggregate columns and the non-aggregate columns that need to be listed in the output.
2. Enter the `SELECT` clause followed by the list of columns to be displayed in the output.
3. If required, enter the aggregate function along with the column names.
4. Enter the `FROM` clause followed by the table name.
5. If necessary, enter the `WHERE` clause to search for the records based on a condition.
6. Enter the `GROUP BY` clause to group the output based on a non-aggregate column.
7. Enter the `HAVING` clause followed by a condition that uses an aggregate value.
8. If necessary, include the `ORDER BY` clause to arrange the output in either the ascending or the descending order.
9. Execute the query.

ACTIVITY 4-4

Filtering Grouped Data

Before You Begin:

1. On the **Standard** toolbar, click **New Query** to open the **Query Editor** window.
2. On the **SQL Editor** toolbar, ensure that the OGCBooks database is selected from the **Available Databases** drop-down list.

Scenario:

The management wants to increase by 10 percent the production of books that have sold 300 copies or more. The publishing department requires the part number of these books so that they can increase the production of the specified books. As an incentive, the management decides to provide a bonus for representatives who have sold 300 copies. The financial department requires the IDs of these representatives to deposit the bonus. For information on the tables and column names in the OGCBooks database, refer to the table structure in Appendix A.

What You Do	How You Do It

1. **True or False? To retrieve books that have sold more than 500 copies, you need to calculate the sum of the sales quantity of the books with the same part number.**

   ✓ True

   __ False

2. Identify the book part number and the representative IDs for the titles that have sold 500 copies or more. Eliminate the rows that have null values as the quantity.

a. Enter the `SELECT` statement followed by the *`FROM`* clause to display the part number, representative ID, and the sum of quantity from the "sales" table. Use the alias name "total_qty" for the sum of the quantity column.

b. Enter the `WHERE` clause to eliminate the rows that have null values in the "qty" column.

c. Enter the `GROUP BY` clause to group the data based on the part number of the book and the representative ID.

d. Enter the `HAVING` clause with the aggregate condition, sum of quantity is greater than or equal to 500.

See Code Sample 1.

e. Execute the query.

f. In the **Results** pane, observe that the part number of the books and the representative IDs for the titles that have sold 500 or more copies are displayed.

g. Close the **Query Editor** window without saving the query.

Code Sample 1

```
SELECT partnum, repid, SUM(qty) total_qty FROM sales
WHERE qty IS NOT NULL
GROUP BY partnum, repid
HAVING SUM(qty) >= 500
```

TOPIC E

Summarize Grouped Data

In the previous topic, you filtered grouped data using an aggregate condition. After you have grouped data, you may find that creating additional subgroups in the grouped data will be helpful. In this topic, you will summarize grouped data.

For a survey on how many people have a Masters degree in an organization, you need to identify and group the information available in the table based on their area of specialization. After grouping, you obtained the count for each group. You then realized that a total number of people who have a Masters degree is also required. This grand total can be calculated by summarizing the grouped data.

The CUBE and ROLLUP Operators

The CUBE and ROLLUP Operators

Definition:

CUBE and ROLLUP are operators that are used to display the summary rows along with the rows displayed by the `GROUP BY` clause. The `CUBE` or `ROLLUP` operator is entered after the `GROUP BY` clause. In the result, the left column value of the summary row is displayed as `NULL` and the right column value contains the summary value.

When the `CUBE` operator is used, the number of columns listed in the `GROUP BY` clause determines the number of summary rows displayed in the output. A summary row is returned for every group and subgroup in the output. So, the number of rows in the output is the same, regardless of the order in which the grouping columns are specified. When the `ROLLUP` operator is used, groups are summarized in the hierarchical order, from the lowest level in the group to the highest. The group hierarchy is determined by the order in which the grouping columns are specified. Changing the order of the grouping columns can affect the number of rows displayed in the output.

Example: Using the CUBE Operator

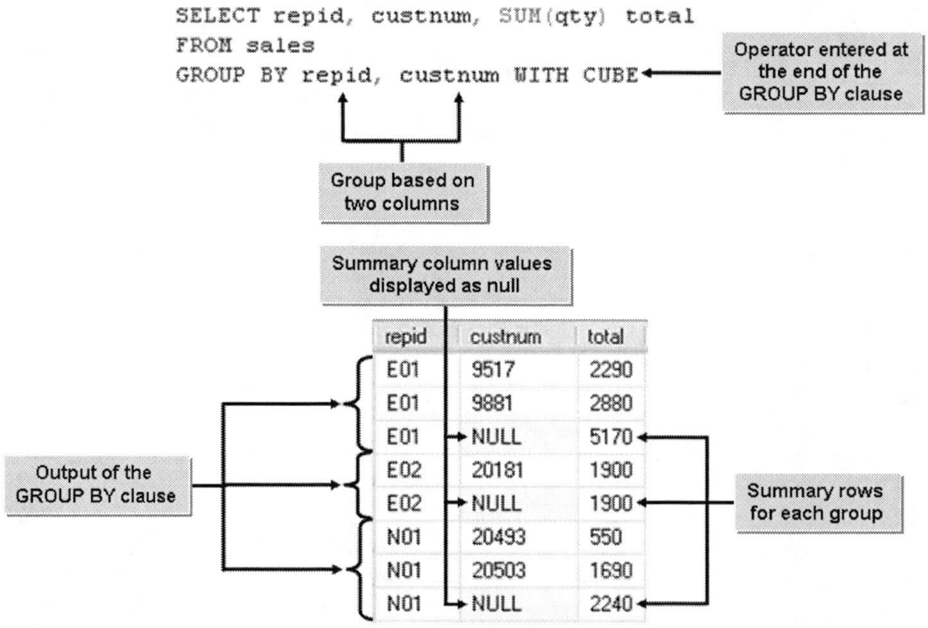


```
SELECT repid, custnum, SUM(qty) total
FROM sales
GROUP BY repid, custnum WITH CUBE
```

repid	custnum	total
E01	9517	2290
E01	9881	2880
E01	NULL	5170
E02	20181	1900
E02	NULL	1900
N01	20493	550
N01	20503	1690
N01	NULL	2240

Example: Using the ROLLUP Operator

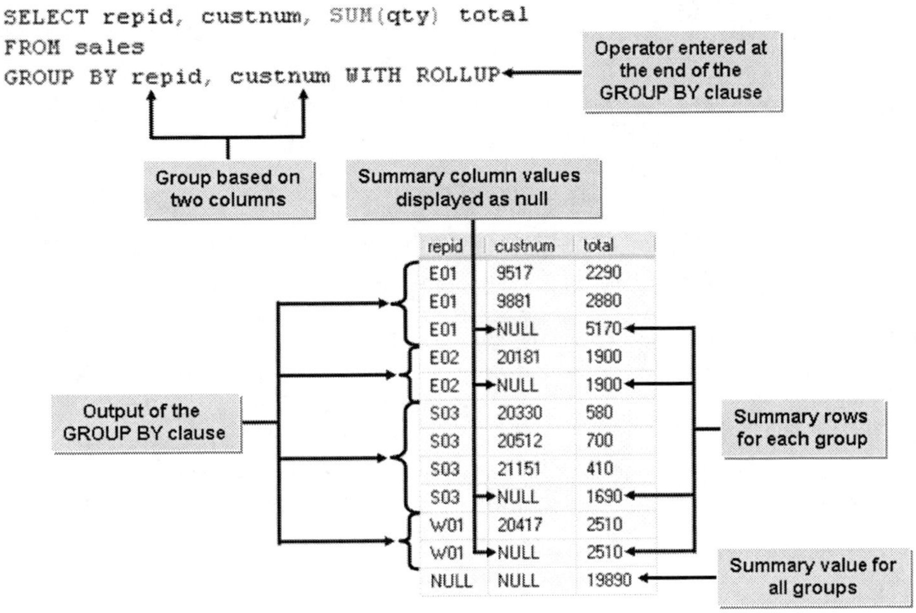

How to Summarize Grouped Data

Procedure Reference: Summarize Grouped Data

To summarize grouped data:

1. Enter the `SELECT` clause followed by the column names and the aggregate functions that are required.
2. If necessary, enter column aliases for the column names.
3. Enter the `FROM` clause followed by the table name.
4. If necessary, enter the `WHERE` clause followed by a condition.
5. Enter the `GROUP BY` clause followed by the column name or the aggregate function to group the records.
6. Enter the `WITH CUBE` operator after the column name in the `GROUP BY` clause.
7. If necessary, enter the `ORDER BY` clause to order the output.
8. Execute the query.

ACTIVITY 4-5

Summarizing Grouped Data

Before You Begin:

1. On the **Standard** toolbar, click **New Query** to open the **Query Editor** window.
2. On the **SQL Editor** toolbar, ensure that the OGCBooks database is selected from the **Available Databases** drop-down list.

Scenario:

To evaluate the performance of sales representatives in a publishing company, data about the total sales made by each representative is required. The query output should list the representative IDs along with the sum of the sale quantity made by each representative and the grand total of sales made by all the representatives. For information on the tables and column names in the OGCBooks database, refer to the table structure in Appendix A.

What You Do	How You Do It

1. **Which operator returns a summary row for every group and subgroup in the output?**
   a) GROUP WITH
   ✓ b) WITH CUBE
   c) ROLLUP

2. Display the representative IDs and the total sales made by each representative.

a. Enter the `SELECT` statement to retrieve the representative IDs and the sum of the quantity sold from the "sales" table. Use the alias name "tot_sales" for the sum of quantity column.

b. Enter the `GROUP BY` clause to return the grand total of sales made by all the representatives.

See Code Sample 1.

c. Execute the query.

d. In the **Results** pane, observe that the representative IDs and their respective total sales are displayed. Also observe that the grand total of sales made by all the representatives is displayed in the last row.

e. Close the **Query Editor** window without saving the query.

Code Sample 1

```
SELECT repid, sum(qty) tot_qty
FROM sales
GROUP BY repid WITH CUBE
```

TOPIC F
Use PIVOT and UNPIVOT Operators

In the previous topic, you summarized data using CUBE and ROLLUP operators. After you have summarized data, you may wish to rotate the column values into multiple columns so as to perform aggregate functions on any columns that are required in the output. You may also wish to rotate those columns into column values again. In this topic, you will use PIVOT and UNPIVOT relational operators.

Imagine that you would like to calculate the number of monitors and CPUs sold by each of the sales representatives in a company. You decide to segregate the number of monitors and CPUs into columns listed against the name of the representatives involved. The PIVOT and UNPIVOT relational operators will help perform this function.

The PIVOT and UNPIVOT Operators

The PIVOT and UNPIVOT Operators

Definition:

PIVOT and *UNPIVOT* are relational operators that are used to rearrange the related columns and values of a table. The *PIVOT* relational operator rotates the unique values from one column of a table into multiple columns in the output in order to perform aggregate functions on any of the columns and display the resultant data in a pivoted table. The *UNPIVOT* operator performs just the opposite of what the `PIVOT` operator does by rotating multiple columns into values of a single column.

Example: Using the PIVOT Operator to Rotate Column Values

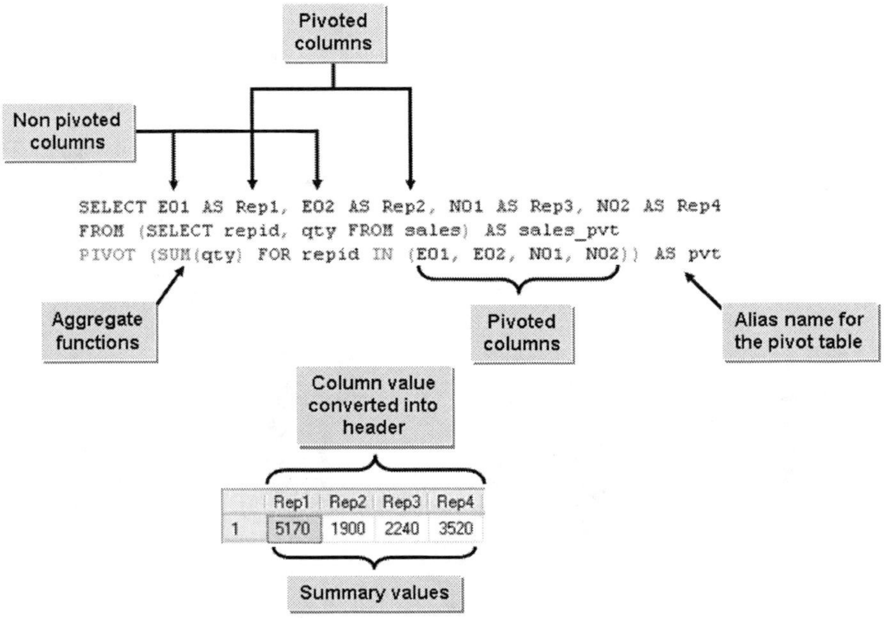

The UNPIVOT Operator

The `UNPIVOT` operator does not perform the exact reverse of the `PIVOT` operator, because the `UNPIVOT` operator rearranges the pivoted column values into columns having new headings and new data.

Syntax of the PIVOT Operator

The syntax of a PIVOT operator is:

```
SELECT [non-pivoted column] AS <column name>, ...[last pivoted column] AS <>
column name
FROM (SELECT query that produces data) AS <alias for the source query>
PIVOT (
<aggregate function> (column being aggregated)
FOR [column that contains the values that will become column headers] IN
([first pivoted column],....[last pivoted column])
) AS <>alias for he pivot table>
<optional ORDER BY clause>
```

How to Use PIVOT and UNPIVOT Operators

Procedure Reference: Use PIVOT and UNPIVOT Operators

To use PIVOT and UNPIVOT operators:

1. Enter the `SELECT` statement followed by column names whose values will be pivoted into columns in the output.
2. Enter the `FROM` clause followed by the table name.
3. Enter the `PIVOT` operator followed by an aggregate function and the columns being aggregated.
4. Enter the alias name for the pivot table.
5. If necessary, enter an `ORDER By` clause.
6. Execute the query.
7. The `UNPIVOT` operator may be implemented in the same way as the PIVOT operator after entering the UNPIVOT operator followed by an aggregate function and the columns being aggregated.

ACTIVITY 4-6

Using PIVOT and UNPIVOT Operators

Data Files:

sales_report.sql

Before You Begin:

1. In the **C:\085971Data** folder, open the sales_report.sql file and execute it as per the instructions given in the file.
2. On the **Standard** toolbar, click **New Query** to open the **Query Editor** window.
3. On the **SQL Editor** toolbar, ensure that the OGCBooks database is selected from the **Available Databases** drop-down list.

Scenario:

A marketing firm maintains a database containing information about the sales representatives and the total quantity of computer peripherals sold by each of the representatives. The accounts manager wants a list of each of the peripherals sold by various representatives. You have decided to use relational operators to generate cross-tabulation reports to determine the number of peripherals sold by each representative.

What You Do	How You Do It
1. Change the column values into column headers and summarize the sales quantity from the "sales_report" table.	a. Type **`SELECT pvt.* INTO sales_pvt`** and press **Enter.** b. Type **`FROM sales_report`** and press **Enter.** c. Type **`PIVOT (SUM(quantity) FOR product IN (Monitor,CPU)) AS pvt`** and press **Enter.** *See Code Sample 1.* d. Execute the query. e. In the **Results** pane, on the **Messages** tab, observe that the message "(2 row(s) affected)" is displayed.

Code Sample 1

```
SELECT pvt.* INTO Sales_pvt
FROM sales_report
PIVOT (SUM(quantity) FOR product IN (Monitor, CPU)) AS pvt
```

2. View the content of the "sales_pvt" table.

a. In the **Editor** pane, type **`SELECT * FROM sales_pvt`**

b. Hold down **Shift** and click before `SELECT` to select the query.

c. Execute the query.

d. In the **Results** pane, observe that the column values "Monitor" and "CPU" have been rotated into column headers along with corresponding aggregate values of the quantity for each representative.

---

3. Change the column headers into column values from the "sales_pvt" table.

a. Press **End** and press **Enter.**

b. Type **`SELECT unpvt.rep_name, unpvt.product, unpvt.quantity FROM sales_pvt`** and press **Enter.**

c. Type **`UNPIVOT (quantity FOR product IN (Monitor, CPU)) AS unpvt`**

See Code Sample 2.

d. Select the `UNPIVOT` query and execute it.

e. In the **Results** pane, observe that the column headers are rotated back to column values.

f. Close the **Query Editor** window without saving the query.

Code Sample 2

```
SELECT unpvt.rep_name, unpvt.product, unpvt.quantity FROM sales_pvt
UNPIVOT (quantity FOR product IN (Monitor, CPU)) AS unpvt
```

Lesson 4 Follow-up

In this lesson, you sorted and grouped the data so that the required output is displayed. Sorting lists the values in either the ascending or the descending order. For grouping the records, you entered search conditions based on aggregate values using the `HAVING` clause.

1. **What is the purpose of sorting the output?**

   Answers will vary.

2. **When would you group the data in a table?**

   Answers will vary.

5 Retrieving Data from Tables

Lesson Time: 1 hour(s)

Lesson Objectives:

In this lesson, you will retrieve data from tables.

You will:

- Combine results obtained from two queries to get a single output.
- Compare results of two queries to get distinct values.
- Retrieve data by joining tables.
- Check for unmatched records in the query output.
- Retrieve information from a single table using joins.

Introduction

So far, you have been retrieving and organizing data using various clauses and functions in SQL. For various reasons, the data may be split and saved in multiple tables within the database. To obtain specific information for multiple tables, you may need to combine the information present in these tables. Sometimes, information from a single table may not be retrieved by using simple conditions. To retrieve this information, you may wish to combine that particular table with itself. In this lesson, you will retrieve data from tables.

Information stored in a database is typically split into multiple tables. For example, in a large database, the employee ID and the order number may be present in one table, and the employee ID along with the employee name may be in another table. Given the order number, to retrieve the employee name, you need to identify the employee ID corresponding to the order number in the first table. Using this employee ID, you can then retrieve the employee name from the second table.

TOPIC A

Combine Results of Two Queries

You retrieved data using a query. Sometimes, you get the result from two different queries. Instead of retrieving two different outputs, you may need to get the output as a single list. In this topic, you will combine results obtained from two queries.

Consider a banking database in which the debit and credit transactions are stored in separate tables. If both the debit and credit transactions of a customer are required, you would need to enter two queries. If the output of the two queries is similar, you can combine the outputs and list them as a single output that lists the transactions of a customer.

The UNION Operator

The UNION Operator

Definition:

The *UNION operator* is used to combine the results of two or more queries into a single output. The `UNION` operator is entered between SQL statements. The number of columns in each query must be identical. In each query, the data type of the respective columns must be compatible. By default, when the `UNION` operator is used, duplicate rows in each query or different queries are removed from the result. To display these duplicate rows, the `ALL` operator is entered after the `UNION` operator.

Syntax of the UNION Operator

```
query_expression
UNION [ALL]
query_expression
[UNION [ALL]]
```

`query_expression` is a query that returns the data to be combined with the result of another query.

Example: Using the UNION Operator

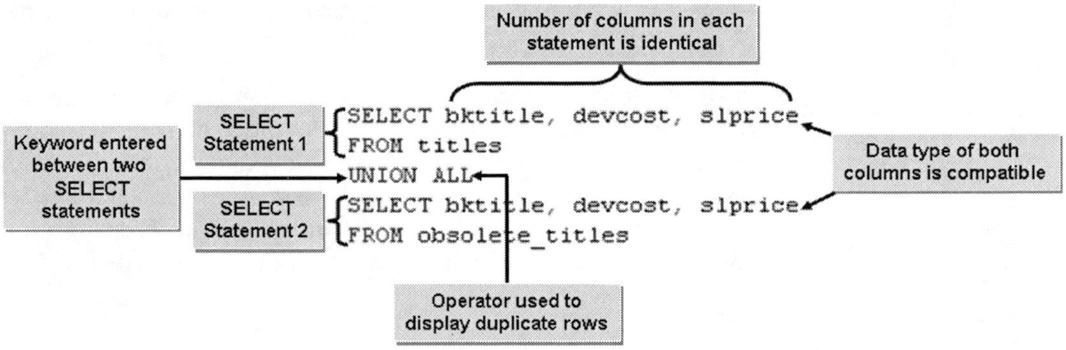

How to Combine Results of Two Queries

Procedure Reference: Combine Results of Two Queries

To combine the results of two queries:

1. Enter the `SELECT` statement to retrieve the column values from the first table.
2. If necessary, enter a condition in the `WHERE` clause to retrieve selected rows.
3. Enter the `UNION` operator.
4. Enter the second `SELECT` statement to retrieve the same column values that were retrieved in the first `SELECT` statement.
5. If necessary, enter a condition in the `WHERE` clause to retrieve selected rows.
6. If necessary, include the `ORDER BY` clause to display the rows retrieved in an ascending or descending order.
7. Execute the query.

ACTIVITY 5-1

Combining Results of Two Queries

Before You Begin:

1. On the **Standard** toolbar, click **New Query** to open a new **Query Editor** window.
2. On the **SQL Editor** toolbar, ensure that the OGCBooks database is selected from the **Available Databases** drop-down list.

Scenario:

To clinch a business deal, the top management wants a list of all books that have been published by the OGC Books publishing company from the day it came into existence. Some of the books that were published are currently out-of-print, and this information is found in the "obsolete_titles" table. The other books published are in the "titles" table. For information on the tables and column names in the OGCBooks database, refer to the table structure in Appendix A.

What You Do	How You Do It
1. List the book title and the publishing date of all the books in the "titles" table.	a. Enter the `SELECT` statement to list the book title and publishing date of all books. Also add the alias names "book_title" and "publishing_date" for the book title and publishing date columns, respectively.
	b. Enter the `FROM` clause followed by the table name to retrieve the records from the "titles" table and press **Enter** two times. *See Code Sample 1.*

Code Sample 1

```
SELECT bktitle book_title, pubdate publishing_date
FROM titles
```

2. List the book title and the publishing date of all the books in the "obsolete_titles" table and sort the book titles by their publishing dates.

   a. Enter the SELECT statement to list the book titles and the publishing date of all books and press **Enter.**

   b. Enter the FROM clause followed by the table name to retrieve the records from the "obsolete_titles" table and press **Enter.**

   c. Enter the ORDER BY clause to sort the book titles by their publishing dates and press **Enter.**

   See Code Sample 2.

Code Sample 2

```
SELECT bktitle book_title, pubdate publishing_date
FROM titles

SELECT bktitle, pubdate
FROM obsolete_titles
ORDER BY pubdate
```

3. Combine the results of the two tables and execute the query.

   a. In the **Editor** pane, click between the two SELECT statements and type **UNION** to combine the results of two tables.

   See Code Sample 3.

   b. Execute the query.

   c. In the **Results** pane, observe that a table containing the book title and the publication date is displayed.

   d. Close the **Query Editor** window without saving the query.

Code Sample 3

```
SELECT bktitle book_title, pubdate publishing_date
FROM titles
UNION
SELECT bktitle, pubdate
FROM obsolete_titles
ORDER BY pubdate
```

TOPIC B

Compare the Results of Two Queries

In the previous topic, you combined the results of two queries. You may wish to retrieve distinct values from the result set of either of the queries or from both the queries. In this, topic you will compare results to get distinct values.

Consider two tables having identical columns containing similar data, except those few rows from either of the tables or both tables containing unique values. When you combine two tables, it will display all the unique data in a single result set. You may wish to retrieve distinct values from either of the table or from both the tables. To do so, you will compare the results obtained from two queries.

The EXCEPT and INTERSECT Operands

`EXCEPT` and `INTERSECT` are operands that return distinct values by comparing the results of two queries. The `EXCEPT` operand returns distinct values from its left side query that are not found on its right side query. The `INTERSECT` operand returns distinct values from both the queries. The two basic rules for comparing two queries using the `EXCEPT` or `INTERSECT` operand are that the number and the order of the columns must be the same in both queries and the data types must be compatible.

How to Compare Results of Two Queries

Procedure Reference: Compare Results of Two Queries

To compare results of two queries:

1. Identify the tables from which you wish to retrieve distinct values.
2. Enter the two desired queries.
3. Compare the results of two queries.
   - Use the `EXCEPT` operand between two queries to retrieve distinct values from the first query. The syntax is as follows:

     ```
     SELECT column1_name FROM table1_name
     EXCEPT
     SELECT column2_name FROM table2_name
     ```

   - Use the `INTERSECT` operand between two queries to retrieve distinct values from both queries. The syntax is as follows:

     ```
     SELECT column1_name FROM table1_name
     INTERSECT
     SELECT column2_name FROM table2_name
     ```

4. Execute the query.

ACTIVITY 5-2

Comparing Results of Two Queries

Before You Begin:

1. On the **Standard** toolbar, click **New Query** to open a new **Query Editor** window.
2. On the **SQL Editor** toolbar, ensure that the OGCBooks database is selected from the **Available Databases** drop-down list.

Scenario:

You are planning to place an order for books that are listed in the "titles" table. However, you've been told by the sales person that this table also contains some obsolete titles, which are listed in the "obsolete_titles" table. You want to ensure that you do not buy obsolete titles. So, you decide to first check the obsolete titles listed in the "titles" table and then list down the titles that are not obsolete so that you can select any of them. For information on the tables and column names in the OGCBooks database, refer to the table structure in Appendix A.

What You Do	How You Do It
1. Retrieve distinct records from both the "titles" table and the "obsolete_ titles" table.	a. Enter the `SELECT` statement to list the book title from the "titles" table and press **Enter** two times. *See Code Sample 1.* b. Enter the `SELECT` statement to select the "bktitle" column from the "obsolete_titles" table. *See Code Sample 2.* c. Click between the two `SELECT` statements and type **`INTERSECT`** to retrieve distinct records from both tables. *See Code Sample 3.* d. Execute the query. e. In the **Results** pane, verify that the book title "Clear Cupboards" is displayed.

Code Sample 1

```
SELECT bktitle FROM titles
```

Code Sample 2

```
SELECT bktitle FROM titles

SELECT bktitle FROM obsolete_titles
```

Code Sample 3

```
SELECT bktitle FROM titles
INTERSECT
SELECT bktitle FROM obsolete_titles
```

2. Retrieve distinct records from the "titles" table that are not found on the "obsolete_titles" table.

a. In the **Editor** pane, double-click the keyword `INTERSECT` and type **`EXCEPT`**

See Code Sample 4.

b. Execute the query.

c. In the **Results** pane, observe that all the distinct records obtained from the "titles" table are displayed.

d. Close the **Query Editor** window without saving the query.

Code Sample 4

```
SELECT bktitle FROM titles
EXCEPT
SELECT bktitle FROM obsolete_titles
```

TOPIC C

Retrieve Data by Joining Tables

In the previous topic, you compared the results of two queries. A single table in the database may not have all the information that is required. The scattered information can be obtained by combining the output from multiple tables. In this topic, you will use simple joins to retrieve data from more than one table.

In an organization, the sales table may contain information about sales and the customer table may contain information about customers. The information that is common to both tables is the customer ID. If you need information about a customer who is involved in a particular sale, you need to identify the sales record and then retrieve the customer ID from the sales table. Then, you need to match the customer ID from the sales table with the customer ID in the customer table to retrieve the information about the customer.

Joins

Joins

Definition:

A *join* is a method of combining data from two or more tables into one result, based on a condition or a column that is common to both tables. There are four types of joins: cross join, inner join, outer join, and self join.

Example: Joining Tables

Column common to both tables

	ordnum	sldate	qty	custnum	partnum	repid
1	00101	2005-11-16 00:00:00	220	20503	40125	N01
2	00102	2005-11-20 00:00:00	100	8802	40232	N02
3	00103	2005-11-20 00:00:00	170	9989	40641	N02
4	00104	2005-12-07 00:00:00	100	9989	40562	N02
5	00105	2005-12-14 00:00:00	150	20493	40481	N01
6	00106	2005-12-16 00:00:00	200	9989	40712	N02
7	00107	2005-12-22 00:00:00	200	9989	40562	N02
8	00108	2006-01-11 00:00:00	200	20417	40125	W01
9	00109	2006-01-12 00:00:00	250	8802	40231	N02

Table 1

	repid	fname	lname	commrate
1	E01	Kent	Allard	0.05
2	E02	Margo	Lane	0.05
3	E03	Fred	Bartell	0.02
4	N01	Richard	Gibson	0.03
5	N02	Pat	Powell	0.03
6	S01	George	Cranston	0.04
7	S02	Amelia	Rose	0.05
8	S03	Charlotte	Matthews	0.04

Table 2

	repid	fname	lname	commrate
1	E01	Kent	Allard	0.05
2	E02	Margo	Lane	0.05
3	E03	Fred	Bartell	0.02
4	N01	Richard	Gibson	0.03
5	N02	Pat	Powell	0.03
6	S01	George	Cranston	0.04
7	S02	Amelia	Rose	0.05
8	S03	Charl...	Matthe...	0.04

Output

The Cross Join

Definition:

The *Cross join* is a join that displays one row for every possible pairing of rows from two tables. In the SQL statement, the `CROSS JOIN` keyword is entered between the two table names that are joined.

The Cross Join

Example: Using the Cross Join

```
SELECT fname, lname, partnum, bktitle, slprice
FROM slspers
CROSS JOIN titles
ORDER BY lname, partnum
```

Keyword entered between two table names

Tables to be joined

	repid	fname	lname	commrate
1	E01	Kent	Allard	0.05
2	E02	Margo	Lane	0.05
3	E03	Fred	Bartell	0.02
4	N01	Richard	Gibson	0.03
5	N02	Pat	Powell	0.03
6	S01	George	Cranston	0.04
7	S02	Amelia	Rose	0.05
8	S03	Charlotte	Matthews	0.04

titles

	partnum	bktitle	devcost	slprice	pubdate
1	39843	Clear Cupboards	15055.50	49.95	2005-08-19 00:00:00
2	39905	Y2K, Why Worry?	19990.00	45.00	2006-01-01 00:00:00
3	40121	Boating Safety	15421.81	36.50	2006-05-18 00:00:00
4	40122	Sailing	9932.96	29.15	2006-05-03 00:00:00
5	40123	The Sport of Windsurfing	12798.32	38.50	2005-07-13 00:00:00
6	40124	The Sport of Hang Gliding	15421.81	49.68	2006-01-06 00:00:00
7	40125	The Complete Football Reference	15032.41	49.99	2005-08-03 00:00:00
8	40231	How to Play Piano (Beginner)	9917.75	25.00	2005-06-11 00:00:00
9	40232	How to Play Piano (Intermediate)	8565.35	20.50	2005-10-22 00:00:00

slspers

	fname	lname	partnum	bktitle	slprice
1	Kent	Allard	39843	Clear Cupboards	49.95
2	Kent	Allard	39905	Y2K, Why Worry?	45.00
3	Kent	Allard	40121	Boating Safety	36.50
4	Kent	Allard	40122	Sailing	29.15
5	Kent	Allard	40123	The Sport of Windsurfing	38.50
6	Kent	Allard	40124	The Sport of Hang Gliding	49.68
7	Kent	Allard	40125	The Complete Football Reference	49.99
8	Kent	Allard	40231	How to Play Piano (Beginner)	25.00
9	Kent	Allard	40232	How to Play Piano (Intermediate)	20.50
10	Kent	Allard	40233	How to Play Piano (Advanced)	20.50

Output containing every row of slspers table paired with every row of titles table

The output of the cross join is called a Cartesian product because every row in the first table will have a relation with every row of the second table. The total number of records displayed in the output will be the number of rows in the first table multiplied by the number of rows in the second table.

If a `WHERE` clause is added to a cross join, it acts as an inner join.

The Inner Join

The Inner Join

Definition:

The *Inner join* is a join that displays the records from both tables that have matching values. The values of the columns being joined are compared using a comparison operator. In the SQL statement, the INNER JOIN keyword is entered in the FROM clause between the names of the two tables that are joined, followed by the ON clause that contains the condition.

Other types of joins will be covered in the next topic.

Example: Using the Inner Join

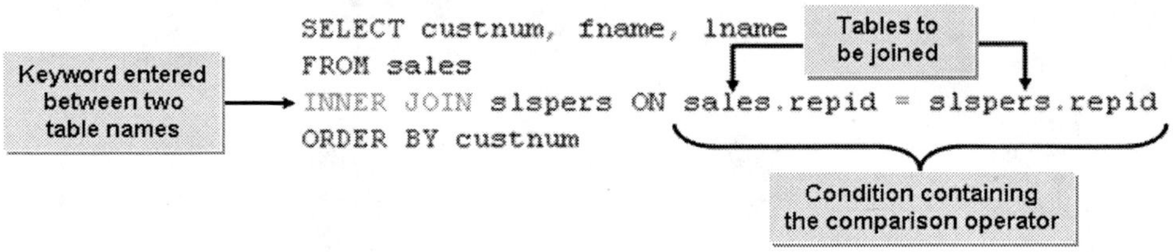
SELECT custnum, fname, lname
FROM sales
INNER JOIN slspers ON sales.repid = slspers.repid
ORDER BY custnum
Keyword entered between two table names
Tables to be joined
Condition containing the comparison operator

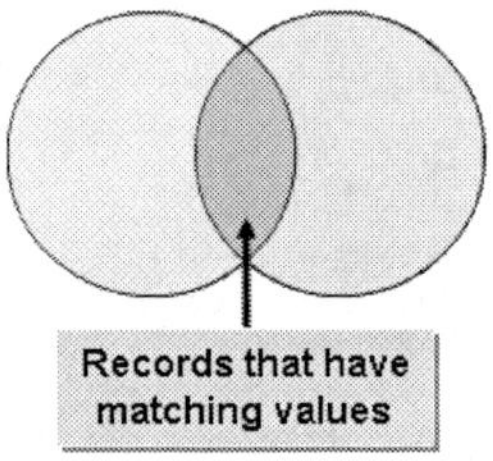
Records that have matching values

Analogy:

Consider a business that employs both managers and engineers, and some people who are both. An inner join is similar to the union of this set: it selects the set of people who are both managers and engineers and provides information about them in both roles.

Syntax of the Inner Join

```
SELECT colname1, [colname2, ...]
FROM tablename1 INNER JOIN tablename2
ON join_condition
WHERE condition
```

> The inner join is also known as an equi-join.

How to Retrieve Data by Joining Tables

Procedure Reference: Retrieve Data by Joining Tables

To retrieve data by joining tables:

1. Enter the `SELECT` clause followed by the list of columns that are required.
2. If necessary, for clarity of output, enter an alias name for each column.
3. Enter the `FROM` clause followed by the first table name.
4. Enter the `CROSS JOIN` operator followed by the table name that you want to join.
5. If necessary, enter the `ORDER BY` clause followed by the column name to sort the rows in either the ascending or the descending order.
6. Execute the query.

ACTIVITY 5-3

Retrieving Data by Joining Tables

Before You Begin:

1. On the **Standard** toolbar, click **New Query** to open a new **Query Editor** window.
2. On the **SQL Editor** toolbar, ensure that the OGCBooks database is selected from the **Available Databases** drop-down list.

Scenario:

To help the sales representatives, the marketing team wants to hand out a list of available book titles along with the part number and the sales price to each representative. The list should have the representative names along with the titles so that it will be easy to identify the list to be presented to each representative. Each representative will get the same list of titles, but will have their respective names displayed on the list. For information on the tables and column names in the OGCBooks database, refer to the table structure in Appendix A.

What You Do	How You Do It
1. **True or False? The CROSS JOIN operator can be used to combine the information in the "slspers" and "titles" tables to list the book title, part number, and the sale price, along with the sales representative names for each representative.** ✓ True __ False	
2. Enter the query to display the representative name followed by the part number, book title, and sale price.	a. Enter the `SELECT` statement to list the first name and the last name of the representatives as a single column without trailing spaces, and "representative_name" as the alias name for that column. b. Enter the column names for the part number, book title, and sale price to be listed in the result set. c. Enter the `FROM` clause followed by the "slspers" table name. *See Code Sample 1.*

Code Sample 1

```
SELECT RTRIM(fname) + ' ' + RTRIM(lname) representative_name,
partnum, bktitle, slprice
FROM slspers
```

3. Join the information with the "titles" table, and sort the output based on the last name of the representative and the part number.

a. Enter the `CROSS JOIN` operator followed by the second table name.

b. Enter the `ORDER BY` clause to sort the columns in the ascending order of the representative's last name and then by part number of the titles.

   See Code Sample 2.

c. Execute the query.

d. In the **Results** pane, scroll down to view the records.

e. Observe that the representative names are displayed in the ascending order of their last names.

f. Close the **Query Editor** window without saving the query.

Code Sample 2

```
SELECT RTRIM(fname) + ' ' + RTRIM(lname) representative_name,
partnum, bktitle, slprice
FROM slspers
CROSS JOIN titles
ORDER BY lname, partnum
```

TOPIC D

Check for Unmatched Records

In the previous topic, you used joins to combine output from more than one table. After you have joined the tables, there are times when you will need to match the records of one table with the other. In this topic, you will check for unmatched records.

Suppose you need to retrieve information from two tables where the first table contains information about books and the second table contains the sales details for the books. To retrieve the information of the sales details that are available for a book, you need to search the book name from the first table and then get the sales information for that book in the second table.

The Outer Join

The Outer Join

Definition:

The *Outer join* is a join that selects all the rows from one table along with the matching rows from the second table. The `OUTER JOIN` keyword is entered in the `FROM` clause between the names of the two tables that are joined, followed by the `ON` clause that contains the search condition. One or more columns can be used to join the tables.

- The `LEFT OUTER JOIN` or the `LEFT JOIN` includes all rows from the first table along with the matching rows in the second table.
- The `RIGHT OUTER JOIN` or the `RIGHT JOIN` includes all rows from the second table along with the matching data in the first table.
- The `FULL OUTER JOIN` or the `FULL JOIN` includes all rows from both tables in the result, regardless of the matching value present in either tables.

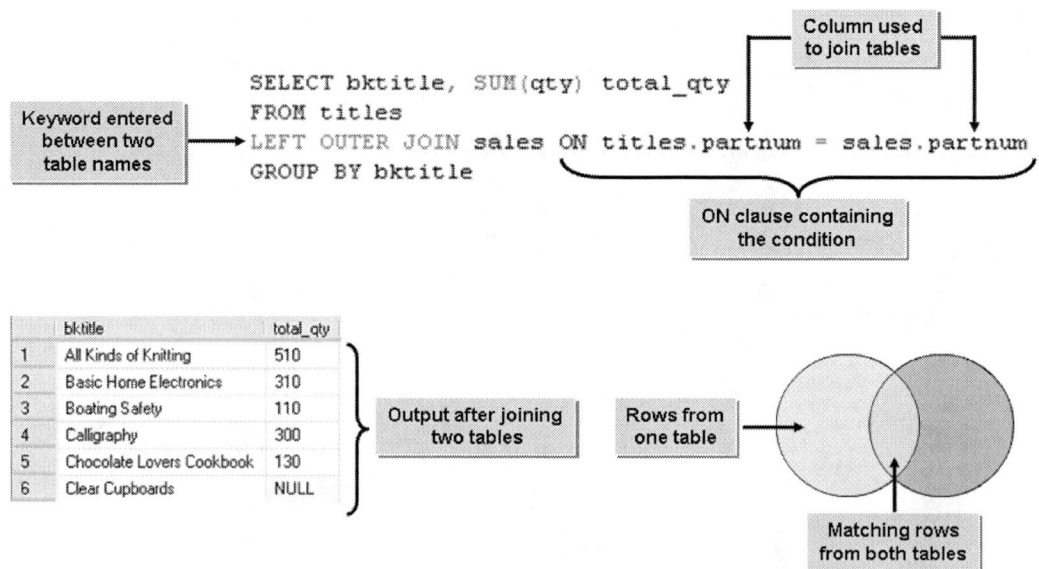

Example: Using the Outer Join

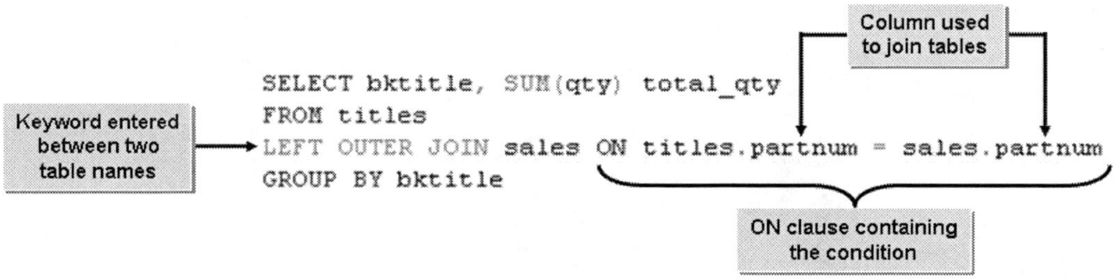


```
SELECT bktitle, SUM(qty) total_qty
FROM titles
LEFT OUTER JOIN sales ON titles.partnum = sales.partnum
GROUP BY bktitle
```

	bktitle	total_qty
1	All Kinds of Knitting	510
2	Basic Home Electronics	310
3	Boating Safety	110
4	Calligraphy	300
5	Chocolate Lovers Cookbook	130
6	Clear Cupboards	NULL

Output after joining two tables

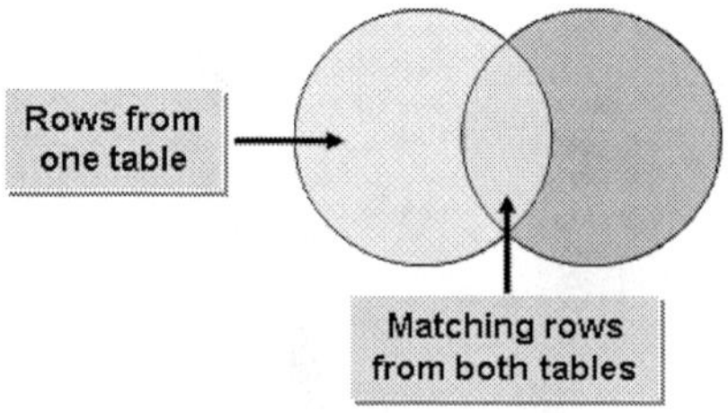

Analogy:

Consider a business situation that employs both managers and engineers. A left outer join selects the set of all the managers, providing information about them, but in the case of managers who are also engineers, it provides additional information about them.

A right outer join selects the set of all engineers, providing information about them, but in the case of engineers who are also managers, it provides additional information about them.

Using Outer Joins Instead of the WHERE Clause

Unlike inner joins, you can't always rewrite outer join statements by including the join conditions in a `WHERE` clause, with the same results. Depending on how you write the `WHERE` and `FROM` clauses, you'll get different results with an outer join. Because you'll get different results depending on how you write such queries, and because such queries rely on the older method of writing join statements, you should not put the join conditions in the `WHERE` clause. Use the inner join and outer join syntax instead.

How to Check for Unmatched Records

Procedure Reference: Check for Unmatched Records

To check for unmatched records:

1. Enter the `SELECT` clause to list the appropriate column names.
2. Enter the `FROM` clause followed by the first table name.
3. Enter either the `RIGHT` or `LEFT OUTER JOIN` conditional operator based on the table, from where the output has to be obtained.
4. Enter the `ON` keyword to compare the columns from both tables to retrieve the records.
5. If aggregate column names are used in the `SELECT` clause, enter the `GROUP BY` clause with the column name to group the rows for calculating the aggregate value.
6. If necessary, enter the `ORDER BY` clause to order the output in ascending or descending order based on the appropriate column values.
7. Execute the query.

ACTIVITY 5-4

Checking for Unmatched Records

Before You Begin:

1. On the **Standard** toolbar, click **New Query** to open a new **Query Editor** window.
2. On the **SQL Editor** toolbar, ensure that the OGCBooks database is selected from the **Available Databases** drop-down list.

Scenario:

The sales team wants to project sales based on the current sales of the titles. To do this, they require the total sales made for each title. Along with this information, they also require the list of titles that have an entry in the "sales" table. For information on the tables and column names in the OGCBooks database, refer to the table structure in Appendix A.

What You Do	How You Do It
1. List all the book titles in the "titles" table along with the total quantity of books sold for each book title.	a. Enter the `SELECT` statement to list the book title along with the sum of sales quantity and press **Enter.** b. Enter the `FROM` clause followed by the table name "titles" and press **Enter.** c. Enter the `LEFT OUTER JOIN` logical operator followed by the second table "sales" and press **Enter.** d. Enter the `ON` keyword to identify the rows in the "sales" table that match the rows in the "titles" table and press **Enter.** e. Enter the `GROUP BY` clause to group all the records based on the published titles and press **Enter.** *See Code Sample 1.* f. Execute the query. g. In the **Results** pane, observe that some of the book titles have total quantity with null values.

Code Sample 1

```
SELECT bktitle, SUM(qty) total_qty
FROM titles
LEFT OUTER JOIN sales
ON titles.partnum = sales.partnum
GROUP BY bktitle
```

2. List only the book titles that have entries in the "sales" table along with the total quantity of books sold.

a. Double-click the word `LEFT` and type **`RIGHT`**

See Code Sample 2.

b. Execute the query.

c. In the **Results** pane, observe that only the titles that have a sales quantity are displayed.

d. Close the **Query Editor** window without saving the query.

Code Sample 2

```
SELECT bktitle, SUM(qty) total_qty
FROM titles
RIGHT OUTER JOIN sales
ON titles.partnum = sales.partnum
GROUP BY bktitle
```

TOPIC E

Retrieve Information from a Single Table Using Joins

Joins are mostly used to retrieve information from more than one table. There may also be times when a single table will have the necessary information, but it cannot be retrieved by just a simple query. In this case, we need to join the table to itself. In this topic, you will retrieve information from a table by joining the table to itself.

Consider a database with the department table containing information about the role of a person and the person they report to. If you want the names of the employees reporting to a particular manager, a copy of the department table is considered the second table for the join.

The Table Alias Name

The Table Alias Name

Definition:

The *table alias* name is an alternative name given to a table so that it can be used to refer to the table without using the table name. A table alias is used when the table name is too long to be repeated in various places in a SQL statement or when the same table has to be referred to as two different tables in the same query. The table alias is entered after the table name in the FROM clause. To access the column present in a table using the table alias, enter the table alias, followed by a period and the column name.

Example: Using the Table Alias Name

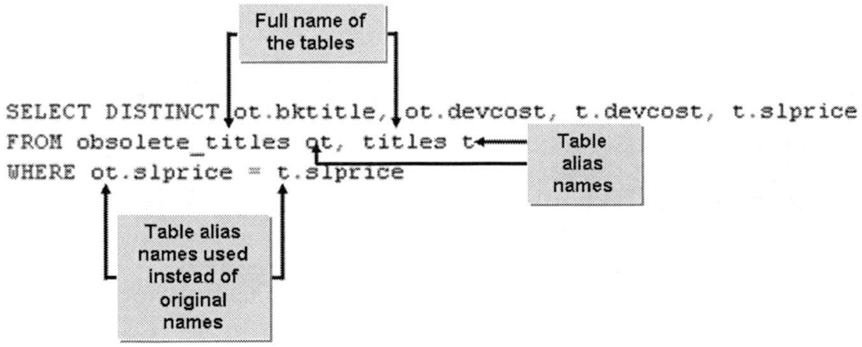
Full name of the tables
SELECT DISTINCT ot.bktitle, ot.devcost, t.devcost, t.slprice
FROM obsolete_titles ot, titles t
WHERE ot.slprice = t.slprice
Table alias names
Table alias names used instead of original names

> The AS clause can be entered between the table name and the table alias.

The Self join

The Self Join

Definition:

The *Self join* is a join that relates data in a table to itself. In the SQL statement, the table alias is used in the condition to identify the table from which the column needs to be accessed. The table to be joined to itself is assigned two table alias names and then referred to as two tables. The `INNER JOIN` keyword is entered in the `FROM` clause between the table names. In a self join, both table names are the same, but the table alias names are different. The join condition is entered in the `ON` clause.

Example: Using the Self Join

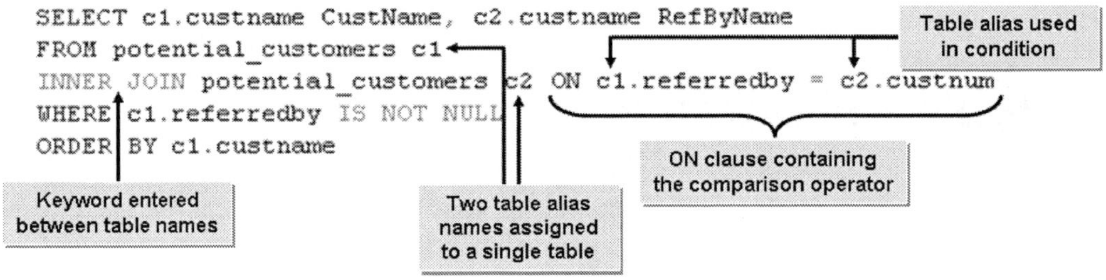

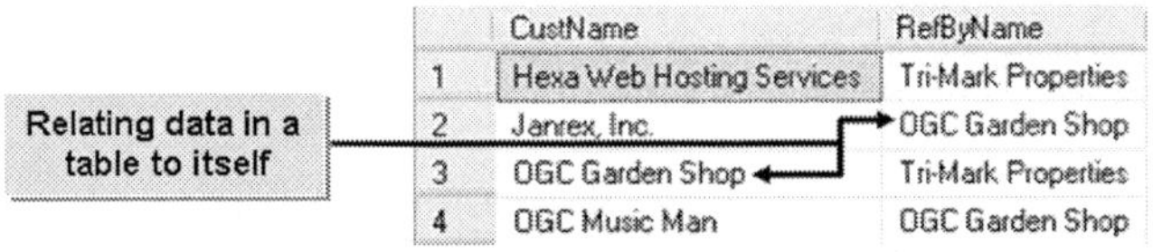

Relating data in a table to itself
CustName
RefByName
1
Hexa Web Hosting Services
Tri-Mark Properties
2
Janrex, Inc.
OGC Garden Shop
3
OGC Garden Shop
Tri-Mark Properties
4
OGC Music Man
OGC Garden Shop

Potential Customers

How to Retrieve Information from a Single Table Using Joins

Procedure Reference: Retrieve Information from a Single Table Using Joins

To retrieve information from a table using joins:

1. Enter the `SELECT` clause followed by the list of column names. For specifying the column name from a table.
   a. Enter the alias name of the table.
   b. Enter a period.
   c. Enter the column name.
2. If necessary, for clarity, enter alias names for the column names.
3. Enter the `FROM` clause followed by the table name.
4. Enter the `AS` clause followed by the table alias name.
5. Enter the `INNER JOIN` clause followed by the table name again.
6. Enter the `AS` clause followed by a different table alias name.
7. Enter the `ON` keyword and then the condition. This condition will equate the column names from both tables.

8. If necessary, enter the `WHERE` clause followed by a condition.
9. If necessary, enter the `ORDER BY` clause and the column by which the output should be ordered.
10. Execute the query.

ACTIVITY 5-5

Retrieving Information from a Single Table Using Joins

Before You Begin:

1. On the **Standard** toolbar, click **New Query** to open a new **Query Editor** window.
2. On the **SQL Editor** toolbar, ensure that the OGCBooks database is selected from the **Available Databases** drop-down list.

Scenario:

Some customers of the OGC Books publishing company have referred others as potential customers. To encourage the customers who have referred others, the management decides to reward them by providing a 10 percent discount on their next five purchases. The future customers will also be provided a five percent discount on their first three purchases. The "potential_customers" table contains this information. For information on the tables and column names in the OGCBooks database, refer to the table structure in Appendix A.

What You Do	How You Do It
1. Enter a query to list the customer names and the names of customers referred by them.	a. Enter the `SELECT` statement to list the customer name from the first table that has the alias c1 with "cust_name" as the column alias and the customer referredby column from the second table that has the alias c2 with "referred_by" as the column alias. b. Enter the `FROM` clause followed by the table name with the alias c1. *See Code Sample 1.*

Code Sample 1

```
SELECT c1.custname cust_name, c2.custname referredby
FROM potential_customers AS c1
```

2. Join the table to itself to list the information about the customers who have referred other customers.

a. Enter the `INNER JOIN` operator followed by the "potential_customers" table name with the alias c2.

b. Enter the `ON` keyword to equate the column values of the two tables and retrieve rows.

c. Enter the `WHERE` clause to retrieve the records that do not have null values.

See Code Sample 2.

Code Sample 2

```
SELECT c1.custname cust_name, c2.custname referredby
FROM potential_customers AS c1
INNER JOIN potential_customers AS c2
ON c1.referredby = c2.custnum
WHERE c1.referredby IS NOT NULL
```

3. Sort the output in the ascending order based on the customer name.

a. Enter the `ORDER BY` clause to order the output based on the customer name column.

See Code Sample 3.

b. Execute the query.

c. In the **Results** pane, observe that four customer names with their references are displayed.

d. Close the **Query Editor** window without saving the query.

Code Sample 3

```
SELECT c1.custname cust_name, c2.custname referredby
FROM potential_customers AS c1
INNER JOIN potential_customers AS c2
ON c1.referredby = c2.custnum
WHERE c1.referredby IS NOT NULL
ORDER BY c1.custname
```

Lesson 5 Follow-up

In this lesson, you retrieved data from tables. When information stored in the database is split into single and multiple tables, and if you need to retrieve information from those tables, you can use joins.

1. **When would you join one table to another?**

   Answers will vary.

2. **When would you join a table to itself?**

   Answers will vary.

6 Presenting Query Results

Lesson Time: 20 minutes

Lesson Objectives:

In this lesson, you will format the output, save the result, and generate a report.

You will:

- Save the query result.
- Generate an XML report for a given query.

Introduction

The result obtained from a query is displayed in the **Results** pane of the **SQL Query Editor** window. A SQL professional would have no trouble in understanding the output. But the results may need to be shown to others who are not familiar with the SQL interface and who may find it difficult to interpret. In this lesson, you will obtain query results in the form of an XML report.

Consider that your boss assigns you the task of collecting specific information so that he can present them in a press conference. But you are not aware of the application that he is going to use in the conference. Server Management Studio Express enables you to save the query results in different formats so that they can be displayed in different applications.

TOPIC A

Save the Query Result

You learned how to query information from tables. After viewing the result, you may want to save the result obtained from the query for future use. In this topic, you will customize the query result and save it.

When the query results are displayed in the **Results** pane, users may not always be able to interpret the column headings. For example, if the table has the column name "bktitle" instead of "book title," the manager who reviews the result may not understand what "bktitle" represents. When calculations are performed on columns, a meaningful column heading is required to interpret the calculations performed to the data in the table. Creating and saving these kinds of query will make the query output more usable.

How to Save the Query Result

Procedure Reference: Save the Query Result

To save the result obtained from a query:

1. Enter the query in the **Query Editor** window.
2. Execute the query.
3. In the **Results** pane, right-click on the blank area and choose **Save Results As.**
4. In the **Save Grid Results** dialog box, navigate to the desired folder where the result is to be saved.
5. In the **File name** text box, type the desired name.
6. From the **Save as type** drop-down list, select the desired option.

> If you want to save the result as an Excel document, select the **Report Files** option. For other file formats, select the **All files** option and type the file extension with the file name to specify the file type.

7. Click **Save.**
8. If necessary, open the saved file and view the content.

ACTIVITY 6-1

Saving the Query Result

Before You Begin:

1. On the **Standard** toolbar, click **New Query** to open the **Query Editor** window.
2. On the **SQL Editor** toolbar, ensure that the OGCBooks database is selected from the **Available Databases** drop-down list.

Scenario:

To analyze sales, the management of a publishing company requires a list of book titles with their corresponding sales figures sorted by the sales value in descending order. This list is generated every month. As the database keeps changing, this list also varies every month. To keep track of the sales figures, you need to save a copy of the query output on the hard disk so that the sales team can analyze the variances of sales when required. For information on the tables and column names in the OGCBooks database, refer to the table structure in Appendix A.

What You Do	How You Do It
1. Enter the query to list the book titles that have a corresponding entry in the "sales" table along with the sum of sale quantity, sorted by the sum of sale quantity in descending order.	a. Enter the `SELECT` statement to display the book title with the alias "Book Title" and the sum of the sales quantity with the alias "Total Sales". b. Enter the `FROM` clause to retrieve data from the "titles" table. c. Enter the *`RIGHT OUTER JOIN`* conditional operator followed by the "sales" table. d. Enter the *`ON`* keyword to match the rows of the two tables based on the part number. e. Enter the *`GROUP BY`* clause to group the rows based on book titles. f. Specify the *`ORDER BY`* clause to display the output in the descending order of the sum of quantity. *See Code Sample 1.* g. Execute the query. h. In the **Results** pane, observe that the book titles along with their total sales are displayed.

Code Sample 1

```
SELECT bktitle 'Book Title', SUM(qty) 'Total Sales'
FROM titles
RIGHT OUTER JOIN sales
ON titles.partnum = sales.partnum
GROUP BY bktitle
ORDER BY SUM(qty) DESC
```

2. Save the query result as a word document.	a. In the **Results** pane, right-click on the blank area and choose **Save Results As.** b. In the **Save Grid Results** dialog box, navigate to the **C:\085971Data\Presenting Query Results** folder. c. From the **Save as type** drop-down list, select **All files (*.*).** d. In the **File name** text box, click and type ***Sales Report.doc*** e. Click **Save** to save the result as a word document. f. Close the **Query Editor** window without saving the query.
3. Open the Sales Report.doc file and view its content.	a. In the Windows Explorer, navigate to the **C:\085971Data\Presenting Query Results** folder. b. Double-click **Sales Report** to open the file. c. In the **File Conversion - Sales Report.doc** dialog box, click **OK.** d. In the **Sales Report.doc** document, observe that the book titles along with their total sales are displayed. e. Click the **Close** button to close the word document. f. Click the **Close** button to close the Windows Explorer window.

TOPIC B
Generate an XML Report

The output that is retrieved from any query is displayed in the Query Editor window. This output can also be saved as an XML file. In this topic, you will learn to save the query result in the XML format.

A SQL programmer can view the result of the query on the screen and analyze the data. But when this data has to be presented in different forms of display, an XML document is a better option. Also, to send out this information to various types of audiences, an XML file, which is code based, would be helpful.

Reports

Reports

Definition:

A *report* is an organized collection of data extracted from one or more tables by a query so that it can be previewed on the screen, printed, or saved as a file. The output of a query can be saved as an XML report by combining the query result with additional clauses available in SQL Server 2005.

Example: A Sample Report

Retrieved from titles table

Book Title	Quantities Sold
All Kinds of Knitting	510
Basic Home Electronics	310
Boating Safety	110
Calligraphy	300
Chocolate Lovers Cookbook	130
Conversational German	400
Conversational Italian	400
Creating Toys in Wood	390
Flower Arranging	200
Furniture Refinishing	240

Retrieved from sales table

The XML

XML stands for eXtensible Markup Language. The XML is used to create custom markups, thereby allowing the users to define their own elements. The main purpose of the XML is to facilitate the sharing of structured data across the Internet. The XML is easily readable because it uses tags, which are self-descriptive. The XML is similar to HTML in its coding format, but is used to define data and not to display data like HTML.

The FOR Clause

The FOR Clause

Definition:

The *FOR* clause is a clause that is used to return the results of a query either as the `BROWSE` option or as the `XML` option. The `BROWSE` option specifies that updates be allowed while viewing data in a database. The XML option can be used to return the results of a query in an XML file format.

Example: Using the FOR Clause in SQL

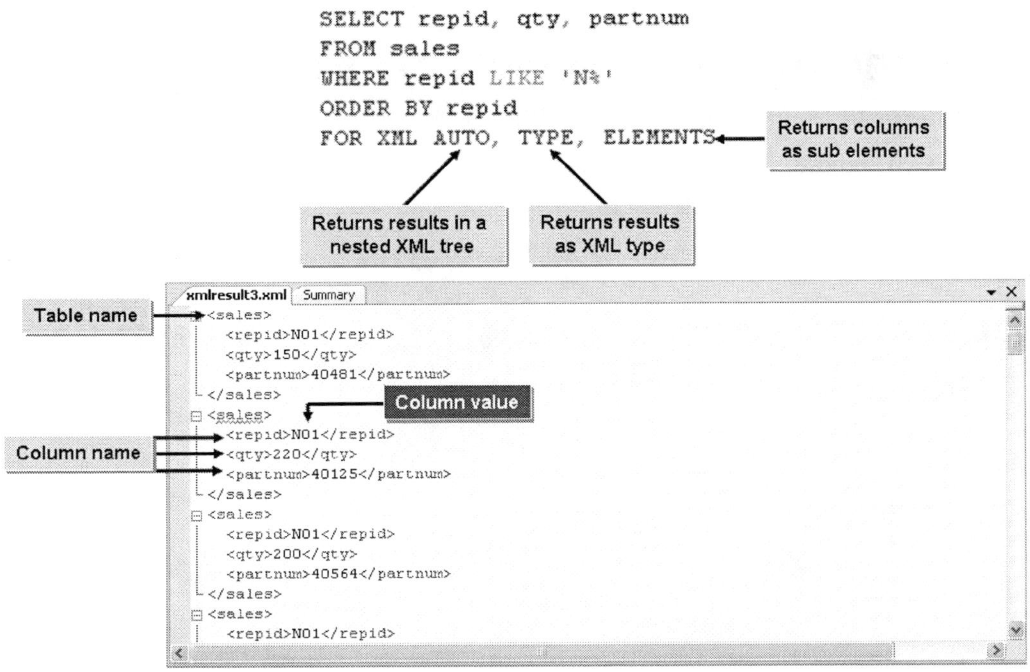
SELECT repid, qty, partnum
FROM sales
WHERE repid LIKE 'N%'
ORDER BY repid
FOR XML AUTO, TYPE, ELEMENTS
Returns columns as sub elements
Returns results in a nested XML tree
Returns results as XML type
xmlresult3.xml
Summary
Table name
Column value
Column name
<sales>
<repid>N01</repid>
<qty>150</qty>
<partnum>40481</partnum>
</sales>
<sales>
<repid>N01</repid>
<qty>220</qty>
<partnum>40125</partnum>
</sales>
<sales>
<repid>N01</repid>
<qty>200</qty>
<partnum>40564</partnum>
</sales>
<sales>
<repid>N01</repid>

Syntax of the FOR Clause

```
SELECT (columnname1,columnname2,....)
FROM table name
WHERE (condition)
ORDER BY (expression)
FOR {BROWSE |<XML> }
```

Modes of the FOR XML Clause

Generally, the `FOR XML` clause requires one or all of the four modes to return the results.

Mode	*Description*
`RAW` mode	The `RAW` mode generates a single element per row in the rowset with a generic identifier as the element tag.
`AUTO` mode	The `AUTO` mode returns query results in a simple XML tree.

Mode	Description
`EXPLICIT` mode	The `EXPLICIT` mode is used to define the shape of the resulting XML tree. It requires a specific format for the resulting rowset that is generated because of query execution.
`PATH` mode	The `PATH` mode generates an element wrapper for each row in a rowset.

How to Generate an XML Report

Procedure Reference: Generate an XML Report

To generate an XML report:

1. Enter the query to retrieve the desired information from the desired table.
2. Enter the `FOR XML` clause followed by the xml attributes.
3. Execute the query.
4. In the **Results** pane, click the hyperlink to display the xml document in the **XML Editor.**
5. If necessary, scroll down to view the contents in the xml document.
6. If necessary, on the **XML Editor** toolbar, select the desired tool to modify the xml document.
7. Save the xml document.

ACTIVITY 6-2

Generating an XML Report

1. On the **Standard** toolbar, click **New Query** to open the **Query Editor** window.
2. On the **SQL Editor** toolbar, ensure that the OGCBooks database is selected from the **Available Databases** drop-down list.

Scenario:

The office assistant has created a query for retrieving the representative IDs that start with "N," along with the sales quantity and the part number of the representatives. This information has to be presented in a versatile file format so that the result set can be transformed and displayed in various file formats. You have decided to generate an XML report so that it can be sent to different departments of the organization. For information on the tables and column names in the OGCBooks database, refer to the table structure in Appendix A.

What You Do	How You Do It
1. Enter the query to list the representative IDs that start with "N" and their sales quantity along with the part number.	a. Enter the `SELECT` statement to display the representative ID, sales quantity, and part number columns. b. Enter the `FROM` clause followed by the "sales" table. c. Enter the `WHERE` clause to retrieve representative IDs that start with "N". d. Enter the `ORDER BY` clause to order the output based on the representative ID column name. *See Code Sample 1.* e. Type **FOR XML AUTO, TYPE, ELEMENTS** to specify the result as an xml type in a nested tree and an element-centric document. *See Code Sample 2.* f. Execute the query. g. In the **Results** pane, observe that a hyperlink containing the table name along with the three columns is displayed.

Code Sample 1

```
SELECT repid, qty, partnum
FROM sales
WHERE repid like 'N%'
ORDER BY repid
```

Code Sample 2

```
SELECT repid, qty, partnum
FROM sales
WHERE repid like 'N%'
ORDER BY repid
FOR XML AUTO, TYPE, ELEMENTS
```

2. Generate an XML report and save it.

a. In the **Results** pane, click the hyperlink.

b. In the **XML Editor** window, observe that all the column values are displayed within their respective column names as xml elements.

c. Click the **Save** button to save the xml file.

d. In the **Save File As** dialog box, navigate to the **C:\085971Data\Presenting Query Results** folder.

e. In the **File name** text box, double-click and type ***Sales***

f. In the **Save as type** drop-down list, observe that **XML Files (*.xml)** is selected.

g. Click **Save** to save the xml file.

h. Click the **Close** button to close the **XML Editor** window.

i. Close the **Query Editor** window without saving the query.

j. Exit the application.

Lesson 6 Follow-up

In this lesson, you formatted query results into an XML report. When you are asked to display a large collection of calculated information as a report, you can use Server Management Studio Express to prepare an XML report that defines the entire data, as well as additional information such as the time the report was generated and details from the company's website.

1. **For what purposes will you save query results?**

   Answers may vary.

2. **Is it advantageous to generate an XML report from a query? If yes, how?**

   Answers may vary.

Follow-up

In this course, you used Structured Query Language (SQL) as a tool to retrieve information from the database. A database contains vast information. You retrieved specific information using conditions. The output obtained can be sorted, grouped, and filtered based on conditions. You also joined tables to extract information present in tables. Then, you saved the query result and generated an XML report using the Reporting Services.

1. **When would you use conditions in a query?**

   Answers will vary.

2. **Why do you need to join tables to retrieve information?**

   Answers will vary.

3. **Why do you want to organize data in a database?**

   Answers will vary.

What's Next?

SQL: Advanced Querying (Third Edition) is the next course in this series.

A The OGCBooks Database

The database used in this book is called the OGCBooks database and is used in a hypothetical book-publishing company called OGC Books. The following tables constitute the OGC Books database.

- The customers table describes each of OGC Books' customers.
- The sales table describes each book sale.
- The slspers table describes each sales person working for OGC Books.
- The titles table describes each book produced by OGC Books.
- The obsolete_titles table describes all books that are out of print.
- The potential_customers table describes any possible new customers for OGC Books.

Table A-1: *Customers table*

Column Name	Data Type	Length	Description
custnum	nvarchar	5	The customer number for each client. Each customer is assigned a unique customer number.
referredby	nvarchar	5	The customer number of the client who referred this potential customer to OGC Books.
custname	nvarchar	30	The customer's name, or business name.
address	nvarchar	25	The customer's street address.
city	nvarchar	20	The city in which the customer resides.
state	nvarchar	2	The state in which the customer resides.
zipcode	nvarchar	12	The state's zip code.
repid	nvarchar	3	The customer's sales representative's identification number.

Table A-2: *Sales table*

Column Name	Data Type	Length	Description
ordnum	nvarchar	5	The order number for each book sale. Each sales order is assigned a unique order number.

Column Name	Data Type	Length	Description
sldate	smalldatetime	4	The date of the sale.
qty	int	4	The number of books ordered.
custnum	nvarchar	5	The customer number for the customer purchasing the books.
partnum	nvarchar	5	The part number of the book being ordered.
repid	nvarchar	3	The sales representative responsible for the sale.

Table A-3: *Slspers table*

Column Name	Data type	Length	Description
repid	nvarchar	3	The identification number for each salesperson. Each sales representative is assigned a unique identification number.
fname	nvarchar	10	The first name of the sales representative.
lname	nvarchar	20	The last name of the sales representative.
commrate	float	8	The sales representative's commission rate.

Table A-4: *Titles table*

Column Name	Data Type	Length	Description
partnum	nvarchar	5	The part number for each book published by OGC Books. Each book is assigned a unique part number.
bktitle	nvarchar	40	The title of the book.
devcost	money	8	The development cost of the book.
slprice	money	8	The sale price of the book.
pubdate	smalldatetime	4	The date on which the book was published.

Table A-5: *Obsolete_Titles table*

Column Name	Data Type	Length	Description
partnum	nvarchar	5	The part number for each book considered obsolete.
bktitle	nvarchar	40	The title of the obsolete book.
devcost	money	8	The development cost of the obsolete book.
slprice	money	8	The price book used to be sold for.
pubdate	smalldatetime	4	The date on which the book was published.

Table A-6: *Potential_Customers table*

Column Name	Data Type	Length	Description
custnum	nvarchar	5	A unique number assigned for the potential customer.
referredby	nvarchar	5	The customer number of the client who referred this potential customer to OGC Books.
custname	nvarchar	30	The potential customer's name, or business name.
address	nvarchar	25	The potential customer's street address.
city	nvarchar	20	The city in which the potential customer resides.
state	nvarchar	2	The state in which the potential customer resides.
zipcode	nvarchar	12	The potential customer's zip code.
repid	nvarchar	3	The identification number of the sales representative in the potential customer's area.

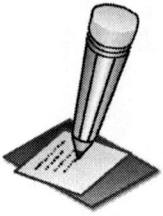

Lesson Labs

Due to classroom setup constraints, some labs cannot be keyed in sequence immediately following their associated lesson. Your instructor will tell you whether your labs can be practiced immediately following the lesson or whether they require separate setup from the main lesson content.

Lesson 1 Lab 1

Writing and Executing Simple Queries

Scenario:

You have joined a publishing company. In this company, information about customers, book titles, sales representatives, and sales is stored in separate tables in the OGCBooks database. Your job is to query this database and retrieve information requested by managers and executives in the company for various business needs. The information most frequently requested by the managers is the details about customers, book titles, representatives, and sales. Some managers have their own preferences as to what information needs to be displayed in the output. For example, the "customers" table contains information about the customer number, customer name, address, city, state, and zip code. But, only customer name, address, city, state, and zip code are required. As these customized queries are requested quite often, it would be helpful to save the queries in a SQL file so that they can be retrieved when the managers request the output. For information on the tables and column names in the OGCBooks database, refer to the table structure in Appendix A.

1. Launch SQL Server Management Studio Express and connect to the server.
2. Select the database you are going to use to retrieve the output.
3. Open a new query window, write the queries to display information about customers, book titles, sales representatives, and the sales made by the company and execute them.
4. Include comments about the output retrieved by the statements.
5. Save the queries as ***Write And Execute Simple Queries.sql.***

Lesson 2 Lab 1

Executing a Conditional Search

Before You Begin:

1. On the **Standard** toolbar, click **New Query** to open the **Query Editor** window.
2. On the **SQL Editor** toolbar, ensure that the OGCBooks database is selected from the **Available Databases** drop-down list.

Scenario:

A sales analysis revealed that most of the books sold were priced between $10 and $30. So the sales manager decides to increase the inventory level for books in this price range. Now, you need to list the book title, part number, and sale price of these books. The sales manager also wants information about the representatives who were hired in the past six months. These representatives were assigned IDs that began with either E or N. The sales manager wants their details along with the list of sales made by them. She also wants the information about the sale quantity made by these representatives if the sale quantity is 400 or above in a single sale. For information on the tables and column names in the OGCBooks database, refer to the table structure in Appendix A.

1. Enter a query to list the book title, part number, and sale price of the books that are priced between $10 and $30. Execute the query.
2. Enter a query to list the sales details of the representatives whose IDs start with either E or N. Execute the query.
3. Enter another condition to the query in step 2 to list the sales details if sale quantity is greater than 400 and execute the query.
4. Save the queries as ***Conditional Search.sql.***

Lesson 3 Lab 1

Retrieving Calculated Data

Before You Begin:

1. On the **Standard** toolbar, click **New Query** to open the **Query Editor** window.
2. On the **SQL Editor** toolbar, ensure that the OGCBooks database is selected from the **Available Databases** drop-down list.

Scenario:

A customer is considered a big buyer if he/she purchases 400 or more books in a single purchase. The sales team wants to identify the customers who are big buyers and list the sales made by them during the first six months of the year 2006. You are also asked to list the total quantity of books sold to these customers and the total number of such sales. There are some customer records in the database with a four-digit customer ID. The human resources manager wants the list of customers with a four-digit customer ID so that she can update the database. For information on the tables and column names in the OGCBooks database, refer to the table structure in Appendix A.

1. Enter the query to list all the columns from the "sales" table, provided the sale was made during the first six months of 2006, and execute the query.
2. Enter another condition to check if the sale quantity is greater than or equal to 400 and list the output.
3. Modify the existing query to list the sum of quantity and count of rows if the sale quantity is greater than or equal to 400 for the sales made during the first six months of 2006, and execute the query.
4. List the details of the customers who have a four-digit customer ID.
5. Save the queries as ***Retrieving Calculated Data.sql.***

Lesson 4 Lab 1

Sorting Grouped Data

Before You Begin:

1. On the **Standard** toolbar, click **New Query** to open the **Query Editor** window.
2. On the **SQL Editor** toolbar, ensure that the OGCBooks database is selected from the **Available Databases** drop-down list.

Scenario:

The sales manager decides to analyze customer demands of the titles in the company. To do this, she wants the total sales of each book present in the database to prepare a handout, listing the books in the descending order of sales. She also wants the list of representatives who have sold 2000 books or above, sorted in the descending order of total sales quantity. For information on the tables and column names in the OGCBooks database, refer to the table structure in Appendix A.

1. Enter the query to list the part number and sum of quantity from the "sales" table.
2. Eliminate the null values in quantity, and group the list based on the books.
3. Sort the list based on the sum of quantity in the descending order and execute the query.
4. Enter the query to list the representatives who have sold more than 2000 books, eliminating null values.
5. Sort the list based on the sum of quantity in the descending order and execute the query.
6. Save the queries as ***Sort Groups.sql.***

Lesson 5 Lab 1

Combining Tables to Retrieve Information

Before You Begin:

1. On the **Standard** toolbar, click **New Query** to open a new **Query Editor** window.
2. On the **SQL Editor** toolbar, ensure that the OGCBooks database is selected from the **Available Databases** drop-down list.

Scenario:

It is the holiday season and the marketing department has decided to send out discount coupons to the customers and potential customers associated with the OGC Books publishing company. You need to list the customer name and the address of the customer. The customer address should contain the address, city, state, and zip code. For an organization-wide internal audit, the auditor has requested the information in the sales table to include the details of the order number, customer name, book title, representative name, and quantity sold. For information on the tables and column names in the OGCBooks database, refer to the table structure in Appendix A.

1. Enter the first query to retrieve the customer name and address of the customers listed in the "customers" table.
2. Combine the result of the first query with the customer name and address of the customers listed in the "potential_customers" table and execute the query.
3. Enter the query to list the order number, customer name, book title, representative name, and quantity.
4. Combine the tables to retrieve the customer name from the "customers" table, book title from the "titles" table, and the representative name from the "slspers" table, and execute the query.
5. Save the queries as ***Combine Tables To Retrieve Information.sql.***

Lesson 6 Lab 1

Generating a Report

Before You Begin:

1. On the **Standard** toolbar, click **New Query** to open the **Query Editor** window.
2. On the **SQL Editor** toolbar, ensure that the OGCBooks database is selected from the **Available Databases** drop-down list.

Scenario:

Your sales manager wants to display the book titles along with their sale price and development cost, which is not null. After viewing the output, the sales manager wants to save the output as .doc and XML reports. For information on the tables and column names in the OGCBooks database, refer to the table structure in Appendix A.

1. Enter the query to display the book titles along with their respective development cost and sale price.
2. Eliminate the null values in development cost, and list the book titles in the ascending order.
3. Execute the query.
4. Save the result as ***Books.doc.***
5. Add options to display the result as an XML document.
6. Save the result as ***Books.xml.***
7. Save the queries as ***Generating a Report.sql.***

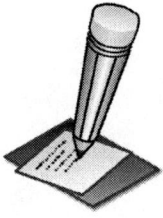

Glossary

aggregate function
A function that performs calculations on a set of values and returns a single value.

AND operator
A logical operator that returns TRUE only if both conditions are true.

arithmetic operators
Symbols used to perform mathematical calculations.

BETWEEN..AND operator
An operator that searches for an inclusive range of values specified by the start and end values.

character extraction
The process of extracting certain characters from a string value.

client
A computer that has applications to use the services provided by the server.

column alias
A meaningful name assigned to the column heading when the output is displayed.

comment
A non-executable set of words or statements describing the intent of the code.

Comparison operators
Symbols used to compare two expressions or values.

concatenation
A process of combining two string expressions into one string expression.

condition
A search criteria used to retrieve or manipulate specific information.

cross join
A join that displays one row for every possible pairing of rows from two tables.

CUBE operator
An operator that displays the summary rows along with the rows displayed by the `GROUP BY` clause.

data type
An attribute that determines the type of data that is stored in each column of a table.

database
Data organized and stored in a computer that can be searched and retrieved by a computer program.

date function
A function used to perform calculations on date columns that contain date and time information.

DENSE_RANK
A ranking function that performs the same task as the RANK function, but assigns consecutive rank values for each row within a specified partition in a result set.

DISTINCT keyword
A keyword used to eliminate duplicate values in a list of values.

FOR clause
A clause used to generate totals that appear as additional summary columns at the end of a result set.

FOR clause
A clause used to return query results either as a BROWSE option or as an XML option.

function
A piece of code with a specified name and optional parameters that operates as a single logical unit, performs an action, and returns the result.

GROUP BY clause
A clause used to group rows based on the grouping columns.

group
A collection of two or more records combined into one unit based on one or more columns.

HAVING clause
A clause used to specify a search condition for a group or an aggregate value.

IN operator
A logical operator used to check if a given value matches any value in a list.

inner join
A join that displays the records from both tables that have matching values.

IS NULL clause
A clause that checks if a null value is present.

join
A process of combining the results obtained from two or more tables into one result and presenting it as the output.

keyword
A reserved word used for defining, manipulating, and accessing data.

leading and trailing spaces
Spaces that are present in a column when the data stored in a column is less than the maximum number of characters that the column can contain.

Logical operator
Operators that test for the truth of a condition.

LOWER
A function used to convert uppercase characters to lowercase letters.

LTRIM
A function used to remove the blank spaces before the value in a column.

NOT operator
A logical operator that reverses the result of a search condition.

NTILE
A ranking function that divides the rows in each partition of a result set into a specified number of groups based on a given value and rank them according to the partition.

NULL
A value that can be stored in a column when the value is either unknown or undefined.

operators
Symbols or words used in expressions to manipulate values.

OR operator
A logical operator that combines the output of two conditions and returns TRUE when either of the conditions is true.

ORDER BY
A clause used to sort the rows displayed in the output based on the specified column names.

outer join
A join that selects all the rows from one table along with the matching rows from the second table.

pattern matching
A method of searching for records that match a specific combination of characters.

Pivot
A relational operator used to rotate column values from one column into multiple columns in the result set.

query
A request sent to the database to retrieve information from the database.

RANK
A function that returns a ranking value for each row within a specified partition in a result set.

Ranking Function
A function used to sequentially number the rows in a result set based on partitioning and ordering of the rows.

report
An organized collection of data extracted from one or more tables by a query so that it can be previewed on the screen, printed, or saved as a file.

ROLLUP operator
An operator that displays, in a hierarchical order, the summary rows along with the usual rows displayed by the `GROUP BY` clause.

ROW_NUMBER
One of the ranking functions, which uses sequential numbering to rank each row in the result set. A ranking function that returns a sequential number for each row within a specified partition in the result set.

RTRIM
A function used to remove the blank spaces after the value in a column.

SELECT Statement
A SQL statement used to retrieve information from the tables present in the database.

self join
A join that relates data in a table to itself.

server
A computer that provides service to other computers in a network.

sorting
A method of arranging column values displayed in the output in either the ascending or the descending order.

SQL statement
An instruction written using the required syntax.

string function
A function that performs an operation on a string input value and returns a string or numeric value.

string
A collection of letters, numbers, or other characters in any combination.

SUBSTRING
A function used to extract characters from a given string.

syntax
The expected form of an instruction with clauses and placeholders for the actual elements that will be used in the instruction.

table alias
A name provided to the table so that the table can be referred to by the alias name.

table
A collection of related information arranged in rows and columns.

UNION operator
An operator used to combine the result of two or more queries into a single output.

UNPIVOT
A relational operator used to convert pivoted columns to column values of a single column.

UPPER
A function used to convert lowercase characters to uppercase letters.

WHERE clause
A clause used to include conditions.

wildcard
Characters used to search for patterns within data.

Index